Drawn by G. Garrard, Associate of the Royal Academy.   Etched by T. Morris.

THE
LIGHT-HORSE DRILL:

DESCRIBING THE

SEVERAL EVOLUTIONS,

IN A PROGRESSIVE SERIES,

FROM THE FIRST RUDIMENTS,

TO

THE MANŒUVRES OF THE SQUADRON:

(ILLUSTRATED WITH COPPER PLATES)

DESIGNED FOR THE USE OF

𝔈𝔥𝔢 𝔓𝔯𝔦𝔳𝔞𝔱𝔢𝔰 𝔞𝔫𝔡 𝔒𝔣𝔣𝔦𝔠𝔢𝔯𝔰

OF THE

VOLUNTEER CORPS OF GREAT BRITAIN.

BY A PRIVATE OF THE LONDON AND WESTMINSTER LIGHT-HORSE VOLUNTEERS.

THE SECOND EDITION.

The Naval & Military Press Ltd

In reprinting in facsimile from the original, any imperfections are inevitably reproduced and the quality may fall short of modern type and cartographic standards.

TABLE OF CONTENTS.

Bugle	Close of the sound is the signal	page	19
Cautions	In filing, not to suffer the horses to back, through hurry to file off	sect.	xvii.
	In forming, not to quit the croup of the preceding file, through hurry to form	sect.	xxiii.
	To pull up before quite in place		ibid.
	Front-rank-man not to quit the croup of the preceding file from hurry to form	sect.	xxiv. & xxxiv.
	Rear-rank-man to halt that leader may pass		ibid.
	Not to cut off angles	sect.	xxv.
	Not to fly off in curves		ibid.
	Method of preventing these faults	sect.	xxvii. & lxvi.
	Rule universal for avoiding crouding, or loosening the files	pages	29 & 37
	Method of avoiding justling in facing about singly, in column of fours	sect.	lxxii.
	In increasing front, the necessity of marching slow demonstrated	sect.	xl.
	General cautions to correct irregularities gradually	sect. xxii. & page 37
Charge		page	36
Column	Of sixes	page	2
	Reason why the space should remain between half-squadrons in a column of sixes	sect.	lviii.
	Position of officers leading a column of sixes	fig. 58 plate 12
	Of fours—from centre of squadron	page	18
	To the rear, from the flanks	page	19
	By wheeling by twos	page	17
	Of half-squadrons	page	27
	Of divisions	page	26
	Of subdivisions	page	28
	Impossibility of breaking into column of subdivisions in the manner directed in the Cavalry Regulations demonstrated	page	28
	March of the column	page 30 & 34
Countermarching	Various modes of countermarching the squadron and its divisions	page 30 to 32
	Objection to countermarching divisions in the manner directed in the Cavalry Regulations	sect.	lxxxix.
	Fault of the description of the same in the Elucidation of the Cavalry Regulations		ibid
Dismounting		page	13
Dressing		sect. i. & sect. lxviii.
Echellons		page 35 & 36
Filing	Defined	page	2
	Single filing	page 5 & 6
	Double filing	page 8, 9 &
Forming	From files	page 6 & 7
	From column of fours	page 18, & 20
	Faults usually committed in forming from files	sect.	lxvi.
	Forming troop, rank entire	page	1
	Rear-rank		ibid & 25
	Squadron	page	25
Fours	See Column		
	See Telling off		
Inclining		page	23
Increasing and diminishing the front			
	From files to single files, and doubling up	page	10
	By forming threes from files, and filing from threes		ibid
	By threes ranking off, and forming again	page	11
	Rule for preserving the place in intricate parts of these manœuvres	sec. xlv. notes
	Increasing and diminishing the front of a column of divisions of a squadron	page 32 & 33

TABLE OF CONTENTS.

Intervals	Between the files	page 1 & 7
	Close files—easy files—and half open files	page 1
	Open files, page 1 & 13——Double distance	page 1 & 14
	Between ranks—See Orders	
	Between divisions—See Column	
Linking Horses		page 13
Manège	Different ways in which a horse may be faced about	page 20, 21 & 22
	Voltes and demivoltes	ibid
	Circles of one and two tracks	ibid
Manual excercise with pistols		page 14 & 15
Markers of wheels		page 26, 27, 28 & 34
	Of march in column and new alignements	page 34
Orders	Close order	sect. iv. & passim
	Close to the croup	ibid
	Sword exercise order	sect. 47
	Order (omitted) It is an interval between the ranks equal to one-third of the length of the rank; and is used in dismounting and in parade—Cav. Reg. sect.	
	Open Order	page 33
Pivot flank	Defined	page 27
	Further explained	page 33
Pivot-leaders	Their duty	sect. lxxx. & xcix.
	Shifting	page 26, 27, 28 & 29
	Objection to the direction in the Elucidation of the Cavalry Regulations as to the shifting of the left flank officer in wheeling to the right into column	page 27
	Impossibility demonstrated of the non-commissioned officers' shifting in column of subdivisions according to the directions in the Elucidation of the Cavalry Regulations	page 28
Ranking off		page 5
Standard-officer	His place in squadron	page 25
	In column of fours	page 18 & 19
	In wheeling by threes	page 16
	by twos	page 17 & 18
Serjeants	Their posts	page 25
	Covering standard—rule for wheeling by threes without justling	page 16
Sword-exercise	Position	page 12
	Remarks on performing in speed	page 12 & 13
Tellings off		page 1, 25 & 26
	Error in Elucidation of Cavalry Regulations pointed out	page 25
Threes	Telling off	page 1 & 25
	Wheeling by threes	page 2, 16 & 23
	Centre-men changed in threes about	page 2
	See title—"increasing and diminishing front."	
Twos	Telling off	page 26
	Wheeling by	page 17 & 18
Wheeling	On halted pivots	page 23 & 24
	Of squadron	page 26
	Into column	ibid
	Into line from column	page 29
	Faults generally committed, and rules for avoiding	page 29
	On sliding pivots	page 33
	Objection to the description of, in Cav. Reg.	page 34
	Wheeling backwards	sect. ci.

PREFACE.

An obvious question presents itself on the appearance of this publication, viz. the necessity of such a work, when the public is already in possession of " His Majesty's Regulations for the Formation and Movements of Cavalry." That valuable work is, however, calculated for the use of those Officers of His Majesty's Regular Cavalry to whom the *rudiments* of the exercise are familiar, and it was probably thought that a detailed explanation of them would have unnecessarily increased the bulk and expence of the book. With respect to the *Privates*, the drill is both from their habits of life and perfect leisure the readiest mode of their instruction.

It is otherwise in the *Volunteer Corps*. In these, both the officers and privates have in general the whole exercise to learn.—They do not of course give up their whole time to the practice of arms—they have other occupations—and it is of great consequence to them, that no more time than is absolutely necessary, should be spent in the drill. At the same time, as many of these corps consist of gentlemen, all of them of men of some education, the privates are able to take the aid which books afford. In this view of the subject the following pages have been written. They are intended as a *drill*, as an introduction to the Cavalry Regulations, and in some degree an explanation of them.

Of the plan, it is sufficient to say, that the horse drill exercise has been minutely and progressively detailed; that the errors into which the recruit is apt to fall have been noticed, and that the whole is illustrated and explained in a series of engravings, in which each evolution is traced.

PREFACE

Should the work be found of assistance to the several corps for whose use it is intended, the author will feel highly gratified in having in any degree facilitated the difcipline of a body of men whose services meet with the warmest approbation of the nation.

The flattering notice taken of the first edition of this book by some officers of distinction, has induced the author to hope it may afford some assistance to officers entering into His Majesty's service.

INTRODUCTION.

It has been hinted in the Preface that this work is considered as preparatory to the instructions ably given in other books, and not to teach that which is taught elsewhere. Yet a few introductory remarks on the subject of riding, may not be here misplaced.

Gentlemen, who are much accustomed to riding, on the road or in hunting, are too apt to imagine that if they can sit fast, and govern their horses, all else is matter of mere form and appearance. They are. however, desired to observe, that a regular seat is of importance, not only to the individual, but to the whole rank; which must inevitably be crooked if one single man in it sits with his back round, or head forward. If he turns out his toes he annoys dreadfully the next man and horse, and his spurs must frequently, by justling, be driven into his horse's sides.

A soldier *must* sit with the small of his back hollow, and body inclining a little backwards. The inside of the thighs should be turned towards the saddle, the legs hanging easily with the feet parallel to the horse's sides, and the heels a little lower than the toes—the ball only of the foot in the stirrup.

This position is far from being stiff, for the arms and legs should hang easily, and the body be pliant, yielding to the motion of the horse. It is far from being irksome; for a man accustomed to it, can so sit much longer without fatigue, than one who lounges in any posture he may fancy the easiest: and it is the only safe seat. It should be much used even out of the ranks; and though gentlemen may not chuse to appear in general on the road, sitting perfectly "en militaire," they will find great advantage in practising to throw themselves suddenly into it from other attitudes: because it ought to become the *natural, unthought of,* effort upon every sudden emergency—such as a sudden halt—a start—or a stumble.

The hand should always feel the mouth of the horse, with more or less pressure, according to the resistance it meets with; the wrist yielding like a fishing rod to the motion of the horse's neck, while he carries his head well.

Every gentleman will recollect, that one hand only can be employed in managing the horse; the other being occupied with the sword. With the left hand, therefore, and the legs, he must be able to guide his horse—rein back, passage, or halt him in an instant. The halt and reining back must be effected by throwing the body more backward than in

INTRODUCTION.

the common seat. The former must be sudden, with the hand a little raised, to throw the weight of the horse on his haunches; the latter must be gradual, and at intervals the hand (*not* raised)* easing the horse's mouth at every two or three steps. When the horse attempts to rear (and then only) the body must be forward and the bridle hand pushed forward on his neck, that he may not feel the bit. If the body be not pliant, the rearing of the horse throws the rider back, so as to hang on the horse's mouth, at the risk of pulling him over; or a sudden halt or stumble throws him on the neck. Perhaps this balance and pliancy of body is best acquired by *very cool* standing leaps.

When the horse is obedient to the leg, he must never feel the spur: when the spur is necessary, it must be applied with pressure, not with kicks.

The horses must be taught to stand steady, to rein back, and passage easily, before they can be of any use in the ranks.

With respect to ATTENTION, we must suppose that the zeal which induces a volunteer to give up a portion of his time to the service of his country, will prevent his indulging a carelessness which renders a man worse than useless. The attention is sometimes relieved, by command " to sit at ease;" it must never at any other time relax for an instant. There is always one, and one only point, to which the eyes must be directed; and gentlemen may be assured, that a spectator (of even very moderate military knowledge) can always decide *by looking at the horse only,* whether the rider's eyes are roving. In halts, march, wheel, or charge, every one must be always studying whether he is an inch too forward or backward; and alive to receive the expected word of command. One instant of inattention disorders the rank. It must be remembered that instructions are to be given by the officer only, and no speaking can be allowed in the ranks. Every man is answerable for his own faults only. If those, by whom he dresses, are too forward or backward, still he must dress by them; the fault lies with them, and he does his duty.

For this reason officers should recollect, that when any part of a rank is out of it's true position, if the men are dressed, the corrections should be addressed to one man only. If, for instance, the rear rank is too close, the flank man, or centre man is alone in fault: it is a matter of which the others have no right to judge.

It may seem almost superfluous to mention the necessity of punctuality to the time of meeting. If every man does not make it a point to be *on the spot before* the time appointed, allowing for accidental impediments, which, though he cannot foresee, he should always expect, some will be waited for, or left out.

---

* Colonel Tyndale, in his Treatise on Military Equitation, observes incidentally, that " a horse, when reining back, indisputably carries his weight on his haunches." It is true he does so; but the less he does it the better.

The advantage of a horse's carrying his weight on his haunches in moving forwards, does not apply when moving backwards. There is no danger of his falling on his knees, or giving his fore-legs or shoulders a shock, as in moving forwards or halting: nor are the spring and action of his haunches and hind legs wanted. In reining back, they frequently sink on their hocks, or rise with their fore-legs in the air. The object is to get their hind legs out of the way, making them push the ground (as it were) before them with their fore-feet.

Pl. 1.

Fig. 1.

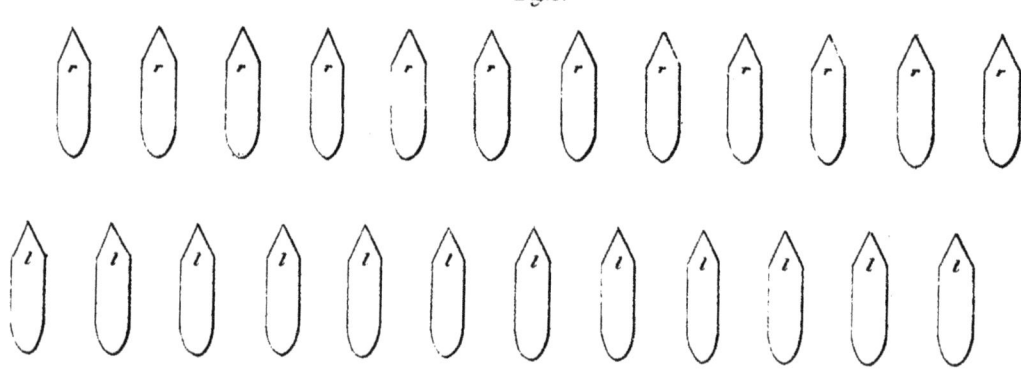

Fig. 2.

Fig. 4. 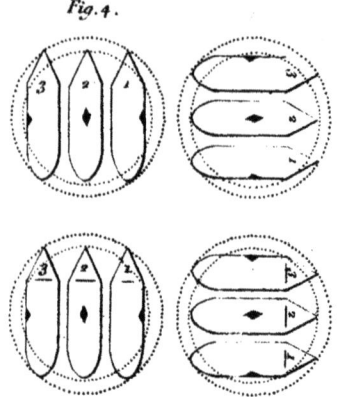 Fig. 3.

THE LIGHT HORSE DRILL, &c.

PLATE I.

SECTION I.—Officer. *Form Troop—Rank Entire.*

THE first man takes his stand upon the ground marked out, and becomes the right flank man; the next upon his left hand, and so on successively in a single rank [*as at Fig.* 1.]

They are to form at *easy files*, or six inches apart; which distance is *always* to be strictly preserved unless otherwise ordered.

They must dress by the right.

Note. There are in use 5 distinct degrees of space between the horses:
CLOSE FILES, or boot top to boot top.
EASY FILES, or six inches apart from boot top to boot top.
HALF OPEN FILES, or a foot and a half apart.
OPEN FILES, or 3 feet; so that a man and horse can just pass betwixt.
DOUBLE DISTANCE, or a horse's length apart; so that every horse can turn on his own ground, or the whole stand lengthwise on facing to the right or left.

The purposes for which these several spaces are used will be pointed out in their places.

In dressing by the right, every man must look to his right, and advance or rein back his horse so as to form an exact line with those on his right: in which case, sitting perfectly upright, he will just see a small part of the face or body of the second man. When he cannot see the second man he is too far behind; when he can see more he is too forward. He must be attentive to this the whole time, whether still or moving; never stooping with his back bent; his eyes never directed to his horse's head, or the ground, or any object whatever other than the first and second man on his right hand, while dress'd to the right, or on his left, while dress'd to the left.

The words of command "*eyes right*" and "*right dress*" signify the same thing. So, "*eyes left*" and "*left dress*;" and must be obeyed smartly and strictly. "*Eyes centre*" dresses those on the right of the centre to the left, and those on the left of the centre to the right: the centre forwards to the officer.

The horses must stand square, (i. e. parallel) and never be suffered to lean, which they will continually attempt.

SECT. II.—*Tell yourselves off from Right to Left.*

The right flank man, with his head turned to the left, cries out, "right" the next turns his head to the left, and cries "left;" and so on alternately through the whole rank. They remain dressed to the left, and every one remembers whether he is a right or left file. [*The letters* r. *and* l. *in Fig.* 1, *and* 2. *distinguish them.*]

Right Dress.

They dress again by the right.

SECT. III.—*Left files! Rein Back—March.*

All the left hand men rein back their horses, to the distance of half a horse's length behind the spaces they stood upon; [*Fig.* 2.] they are not to close; but remain covering the intervals, (i. e. exactly behind the spaces they have left) till the next word.

The officer may perhaps command them to "form up" or "form rank entire" in which case they come again into the spaces they quitted, and again receive the word to rein back.

Observe, that no word of command that requires the horses *to be put in motion* from a halt, is to be obeyed till the word "*march*" is given. The word of command is called the caution: and upon the *caution*, every man is to be thoroughly prepared to perform at the word "*march*." When however they are not halted, they are to perform immediately upon the caution, and no word "*march*" is then given. It is therefore usual (after the word of command has been obeyed) to give the word "*halt*," except where the movements are required to follow rapidly.

B

SECT. IV.—*To the Right, close your Files, and Cover—March.*

The right flank man stands fast; all the rest passage up to the right, and form two ranks at easy files, and at *close order*. The rear rank men covering (i. e. being in a direct line behind) their file leaders, and all dress by the right.

The word ORDER, denotes the interval to be preserved between the ranks; of which there are several degrees for different purposes: viz.—OPEN ORDER—ORDER—SWORD EXERCISE ORDER—CLOSE ORDER—and CLOSE to the CROUP.

CLOSE ORDER, signifies *half a horse's length* between front and rear rank, and is always to be taken, unless the word of command is given for another. There should be clear room for a man and horse to pass betwixt the ranks. The difference between *close order* and close to the croup must be carefully remembered; the flank men are answerable for the interval, when dress'd by the right or left, the centre when dress'd by the centre.

CLOSE to the CROUP signifies, as near as possible *without touching*. Touching must always be avoided if possible.

The remaining ORDERS will be explained in their several places.

Every front rank man has now his *covering file*, and every rear rank man his *leading* file, whom he must take care to remember during the day, as well as every man his right and left hand man; in order to find his place in forming after filing or dispersing.

Note [*filing*]. Men, before or behind one another, are called "*in file*," from the French *filer*; and in this situation can pass the narrowest passages or *defiles*.

Those a-breast of each other, are called "*in rank*," from the French *ranger*, to place in a row. Therefore in the situation described in this section, there are 2 ranks and 12 files. Twelve *file*, (cavalry being formed two deep) signifies 24 men, so forty *files* signifies 80 men and so forth.

Number yourselves from Right to Left.

The right flank man of the front rank turns his head, and speaking over his left shoulder so that his covering file may hear, cries out "one" the next in like manner cries "two" and so on successively. The leading and covering files have the same numbers, which they must carefully remember. [*They are numbered accordingly in fig. 3. and the subsequent figures, and the rear rank distinguished by a small line under the number.*]

SECT. V.

They are then told off by the officer, by threes; right, centre, left; beginning always at the centre of the rank, troop, or squadron, and telling off to the flanks.

Every man must carefully remember whether he is right, centre, or left of threes. Every rear rank man is the same as his file leader.

[*In the figures, the centres of threes are distinguished by a small diamond in the middle—the right of threes by a half diamond on the right—and the left by the like on the left.*]

This division into threes, is for the purpose of *facing*. In the infantry, every man faces singly on the ground he stands on. The form of a horse, does not allow him room in the ranks for that purpose. Three horses (form'd at easy files) occupy in width, a space about equal to the ground one horse stands on lengthwise. They can of course turn all three in a body in that space, by means of the centre man turning his horse on his own ground, while the outsides keep parallel to him; the one moving forwards, the other backwards in the circle described in Fig. 4. This motion therefore by threes, (though always called *wheeling* by threes) is equivalent to the *facing* of infantry.

The following is the remark made on this evolution by Col. Tyndale, in his Treatise on Military Equitation: "Trifling as this appears, it certainly is difficult, for few squadrons ever to do it well. IT CANNOT BE DONE TOO SLOWLY—as one flanker must *wheel backwards* ROUND, which is very difficult."

If the horses are sufficiently supple for this purpose, they ought to move in the *inner* circle described in the figure; whose diameter is equal to the length of one horse. When they are not, they must occupy the greater circle, which comprehends the extreme points. This is one of the many advantages of preserving *easy files*.

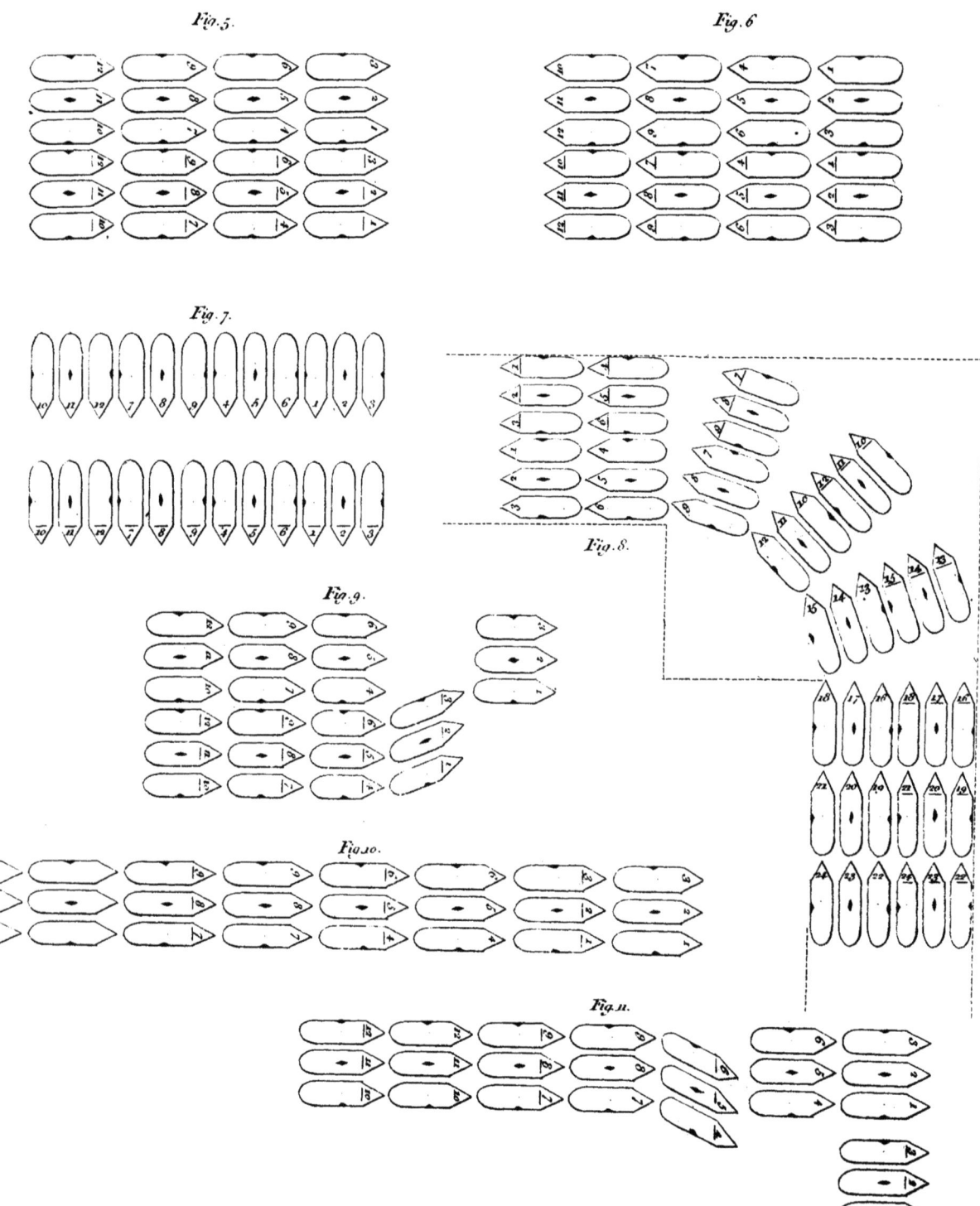

PLATE II.

SECT. VI.—*Threes! Right Wheel—March.*

Upon the caution, the right and left of threes dress inwards, (i. e. by their common centres) carrying their bridle hands at the same time inwards, (i. e. over the horse's shoulder towards the centre horse,) so as to bend the horse's neck in that direction; the centre of threes look to their left-hand man, and upon the word "march" the right of threes all rein back, the centres face to the right on their own ground, and the left move forwards. The turn is a quarter of a circle.

If their motion was perfectly regular, and if the length of a horse was exactly equal to the width of three, there would be an interval between the front and rear ranks, equal to the before-mentioned interval of close order, as there is in *Fig.* 4. Upon the word "*halt, dress,*" this interval must be closed in upon, and the ranks of six a-breast drest by the left (i. e. their former front) at easy files.

[*See fig.* 5. *Where the numbers are shewn in their position, and the right, centre, and left of threes, distinguished by their marks.*

When this interval is closed in upon, and the ranks are afterwards ordered to *wheel up*, it is plain, that if the execution was perfect, the interval must again be wanting. Men accustomed to this motion and used to correct dressing, move so that there shall be no occasion to close in, in the first instance, or rein back in the second; but they get it by practice they know not how. The niceties in the theory of this most useful of all evolutions, are not taught or even any where laid down. It is true that practice is superior to theory, but it is as true, that correct theory facilitates and perfects practice. In this case the fact is, that the motion of the rear rank is *not* the same as that of the front, or if it is, the interval above-mentioned must be closed or opened after every wheel and wheel up; time unnecessarily lost. The centre horse, of a *front rank three*, should turn exactly upon his own centre, the outsides keeping parallel. The centre horse of a *rear rank three*, moves a little forwards in wheeling to the right or left, and a little backwards in wheeling up, throwing the centre of his motion between him and the right-hand horse, in wheeling to the right and back, and vice versa in wheeling to the left and back. In wheeling *about*, he performs exactly the same as the centre of a front three.

The rear rank is now on the right of the front, and the left, or outside of the front rank are now called pivot-men [note]; they are to look every one at the man before him, so as to cover exactly, keep close to the croup, and all others dress by them.

Note. [*pivot.*] A further explanation of this word will be given in its place.

SECT. VII.—*Threes! Wheel up—March.*

Upon the caution the right and left of threes dress inwards as before; but the centres look to their right. They wheel to the left again to their former front, by the left of threes reining back, the centre facing to the left, and the right moving forwards—they dress by the right.

[The position of Fig. 3, plate 1, is now resumed.]

SECT. VIII.—*Threes! Left Wheel.—March.*

They wheel to the left exactly upon the same principle [*Fig.* 6.]

The left flank men become the leaders—and the rear rank is now on the left of the front rank—the pivot on the right.

SECT. IX.—*Threes! Wheel up—March.*

They resume their former front by wheeling to the right.

"Wheel up"—always signifies to resume their former front, whether they stand wheeled to right, left, or right about.

SECT. X.—*Threes! Right about Wheel (or Threes! about)—March.*

They wheel to the right about, in the same way as to the right in Section VI.—only making a further turn, viz. half a circle, and stand faced to the rear. [*Fig.* 7.]

The word more frequently given by the squadron officer, is, "threes about" it always signifies *right* about.

Observe in this figure, the relative situation of the numbers. In fig. 7, No. 6 and 7 are the centre-men of the rank—now No. 4 and 9 are become centre men. In wheeling about, the outside men of the two centre threes, always become the centre men. This observation material in squadron dressed by the centre, as will be seen hereafter.

SECT. XI.—*Threes! Wheel up (or Threes! about).—March.*

To the *right* about always—resume their front, and dress by the *right*. Easy files and close order.

[They have regained the position of Fig. 3, plate 1.]

SECT. XII.—*Threes! Right Wheel—March.*

[See Section VI. and Fig. 5.]

SECT. XIII.—*Forward.*

They move forward on a walk, unless a trot or gallop be ordered; the leading pivot is led by his officer, or else taking two objects in a line before him, by keeping them in a line insures a straight march; the pivot-men looking right forward, and keeping close to the croup—all the rest dressing by them, and covering those before them.

SECT. XIV.—*Right Shoulders forward.*

The leading pivot-man, continuing his pace steadily, turns his horse towards the left, describing part of a small circle; those on the right, keeping their horses parallel to, and dressing by him, describe a larger circle at the same time [*Fig.* 8.] All the successive sixes perform the same *when they arrive on the same ground*—the pivots keeping close to the croup, the rest as nearly so as they can: the leaders continue the curve till the officer gives the word "*forward*," which he does when they arrive in the intended line of march; at which they march straight forward.

It is obvious, that the outside or right hand man, passes over more ground in the same time, and of course must move at a brisk pace. He must take care not to croud or run off, but preserve his distance from the pivot. The track and the pace of all the rest, diminish gradually inwards, from the outside man to the pivot. The angle they make, will depend upon the officer; who gives the word "forward" sooner or later. In Fig. the 8th. a right angle is made—the dotted lines shew the former, and the new lines of march—the numbers also are increased, in order to illustrate it more distinctly. It is common for drill-serjeants to direct, that in "*right or left shoulders forward*" the reverse flank, (i. e. the outside men in this figure) should be close to the croup—ask them how that is to be accomplished, they will tell you, by quickening their pace and inclining—ask them what fills up the interval behind, they make the like answer; and so on through the whole column. Yet they will agree, that the line of every six, is to be correctly dressed by the pivot. It is however impossible that the reverse flank should be close to the croup. The pivot flank forms part of a small circle, the reverse flank part of a larger, and concentric circle; and the several ranks must diverge, for they are the radii. There must therefore be intervals somewhere, and those intervals ought to be (and will be if the ranks are dressed) equally divided by all the ranks occupying the curve. This matter is of more importance in squadron-movements, and a farther illustration of it will be given in its place.

SECT. XV.—*Rear Rank! Left incline and Cover.*

The first three of the rear rank inclines to the left, and falls in behind the leading files; the second three of the front rank slackening pace to make room for them; [*Fig.* 9.] the second three of the rear rank does the like; and so on through the other threes, *as they successively come up to the same ground.*

They march forward in threes a-breast, the threes being alternately front and rear [*as in Fig.* 10.]

SECT. XVI.—*Rear Rank! Right incline, and double your Front.*

The first three of the rear rank inclines to the right, and comes up again a-breast of the front rank. The next three of the front rank closes up to the croup, and the succeeding threes do the like *when they come to the same ground* [*Fig.* 11.]

They are now a-breast again, as in Fig. 5.

When marching from the left flank, (as when threes are wheeled to the left) the rear rank threes, in order to cover, must incline to the *right*, and to double the front, *to the left.*

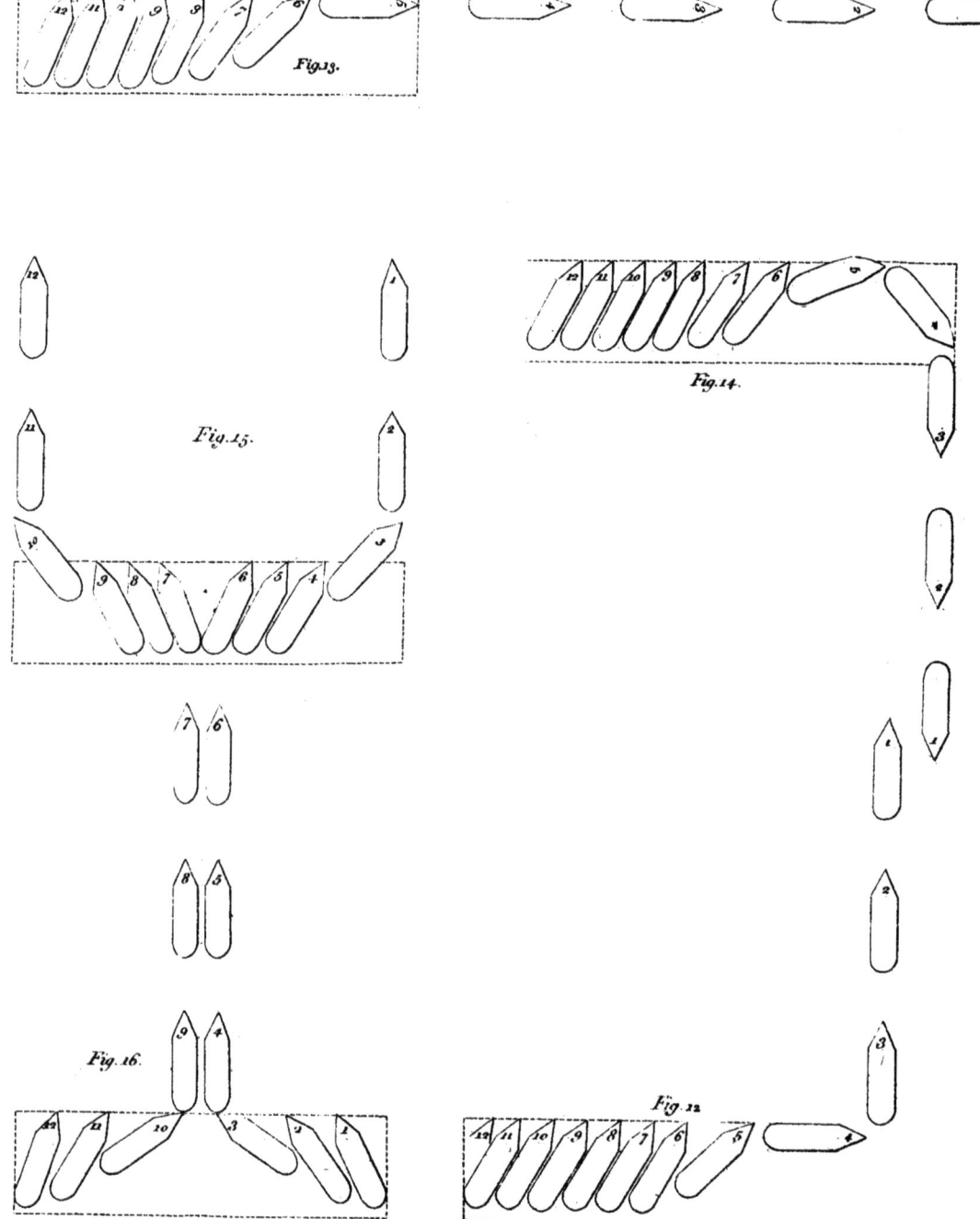

PLATE III.
Filing.

WHEN the squadron is at *order,* or *open order* (i. e. formed with a greater space between the ranks for purposes which will be afterwards explained) " from the right (or left) file" signifies that the ranks should file separately.

When at *cloſe order,* they file off together; unless the word is "*rank off*" or, "*by ranks* from the right file." Even the word *by single files* is obeyed by both ranks together, only the rear rank men falling in behind the front as they go off, so as to form a single file as in Fig. 33.

For greater simplicity, we begin with filing from a single rank; called *ranking* off.

SECT. XVII.—*From the Right File to the Front.—March.*

Upon the caution they all carry their bridle hands to the right, so as to turn the horses' heads the way they are to file. And upon the word "*march*" the right flank man marches forward, taking two objects in a line before him, and preserving that line. The reſt wait each one till his right-hand man has quitted his ground, then follow close to the croup till arrived at the spot the firſt man quitted, where they wheel to the left and follow in the line described by the firſt man, preserving an interval of 3 feet between every horse. [*Fig.* 12.]

In doing this, recruits are apt to back their horses, instead of waiting till room is left them; this presses the others out. It is done through hurry, but time is lost by it, as is generally the case with ill judged hurry. The maxim "*festina lente*" applies strongly to the movements of cavalry. Men must execute briskly upon all occasions: but it must be done without hurry, and so as not to impede others. They are to turn into the horizontal line, (i. e. the line where the horse's *front* was) by advancing each one separately and successively, just the length of his horse's neck beyond that line in order to facilitate the turn, then pass along there, and into the perpendicular, when arrived at the angle from which the first man moved: this angle must be preserved and not cut off in the smallest degree. It must be observed that a supple horse bends his neck and body in turning at the angles: but as the altering the form of the objects in the plates would tend to confuse, and as it is impossible to delineate motion upon paper, some of the angles appear in the plates more cut off than they should be. A soldier must not allow his horse to lean or turn before he is actually *on the spot* where his leader turned, or where (being himself a leader) his orders or his known duty point out the spot for him.

From the cause last mentioned the figures represent too great a degree of *inclining* in the ranks *preparing* to file; which should be executed with no other change of position than that of the bend of the horse's neck.

SECT. XVIII.—*Right File.—March.*

Performed exactly in the same way, only ſtriking off ſtraight to the right inſtead of the front. [*Fig.* 13.]

Keep the like interval as directed in last section.

SECT. XIX.—*From the Right File to the Rear.—March.*

The right flank man turns his horse about, preserves his direction by the like means as in Sect. 17, the others closing up and following him, preserving the angle and the intervals. [*Fig.* 14.]

Filing from the left, to the front, left and rear, performed exactly in the same way, beginning only from the left flank.

SECT. XX.—*From both Flanks File to the Front.—March.*

Those on the right of the centre, file from the right flank; those on the left of the centre from the left flank. [*Fig.* 15.]

SECT. XXI.—*From both Flanks File to the Rear.—March.*

After the preceding sections, this needs no explanation.

SECT. XXII.—*From the Centre File to the Front.—March.*

The two centre men move forwards, those on the right and left side file inwards, turning their horses in line as before directed. [*Fig.* 16.]

The officer names the centre men.

In all filings it has been observed, that an interval of 3 feet is to be preserved between the horses. (Cav. Reg. p. 26.) The least slackening or quickening of pace in front, is apt to disturb this interval all through the line, which tendency every one must endeavour to correct. If he finds his interval is too great, he must close *gradually*; otherwise a jerk will follow all along the line: *by watching attentively the files before him,* he may avoid getting too close, let those before him retard ever so suddenly. Even upon a sudden halt it ought to be avoided by these means, although from the length of the line, together with the noise of the horses, or wind, or from other circumstances, he should not hear the word. In this and all other positions the words "halt" and "march" must be obeyed by all in the same instant.

PLATE IV.

SECT. XXIII.—*Left Form.*

THE leading man simply turns his horse to the left, advancing about a horse's length, where he halts; the next man forms up on his left hand, and so on successively. [*Fig. 17. where the dotted lines represent the ground on which they are to form.*]

No man must quit the line of file, till his leading man is in his place, when he moves up a-breast putting on his right leg *before* he is quite in his place, in order to preserve the space of six inches, or easy files.

He must also pull up his horse half a horse's length, before he is in the line, and move up slower, to prevent the necessity of reining back, in case he overshoots a little.

They dress by the right. *Dressing* is always to the hand formed to.

Observe in the figures representing the forming, those still in file are closed in different degrees upon the intervals mentioned to be always preserved in file, because upon the word "form" they are to come up to the croup.

[Note.] To *put on the leg*, is to press the inside of the foot and leg against the horse's flank—it is used always in passaging, to direct the horse which way to passage, and again on the opposite side when passaged to the place. *The latter is here required: if the horse does not obey the leg, he must feel the spur with it, but this must be given very cautiously.

SECT. XXIV.—*To the Front Form.*

The leading man halts—the next comes up a-breast on his left hand, and so on through the whole line—easy files. [*Fig.* 18.]

Observe, that each man must come up in file to his place, and by no means move up to his leader, till that leader has formed in his place. The whole must follow the exact track of their leaders, and come up one by one, into their respective places in the line.

[*See the Cavalry Regulations,* p. 26.]

SECT. XXV.

Figures 19 and 20 are intended to describe two faulty methods of performing this, frequently practised from hurry.

In the former they are represented cutting off the angle instead of keeping up along the croups. In the latter, they are seen severally coming up a-breast of their leaders from the line in file, and thrown into a curve, by which means much irregularity ensues; besides which, though on a smooth parade ground there may be room for it, on strange ground they may meet with obstacles, unevenness, or pits; and it is obvious that that should be practised, which on service must be performed.

Men in file are supposed to be passing a defile. Forming them immediately on having passed it (as through a gate for example) obliges them to form regularly and impresses these cautions on their memory.

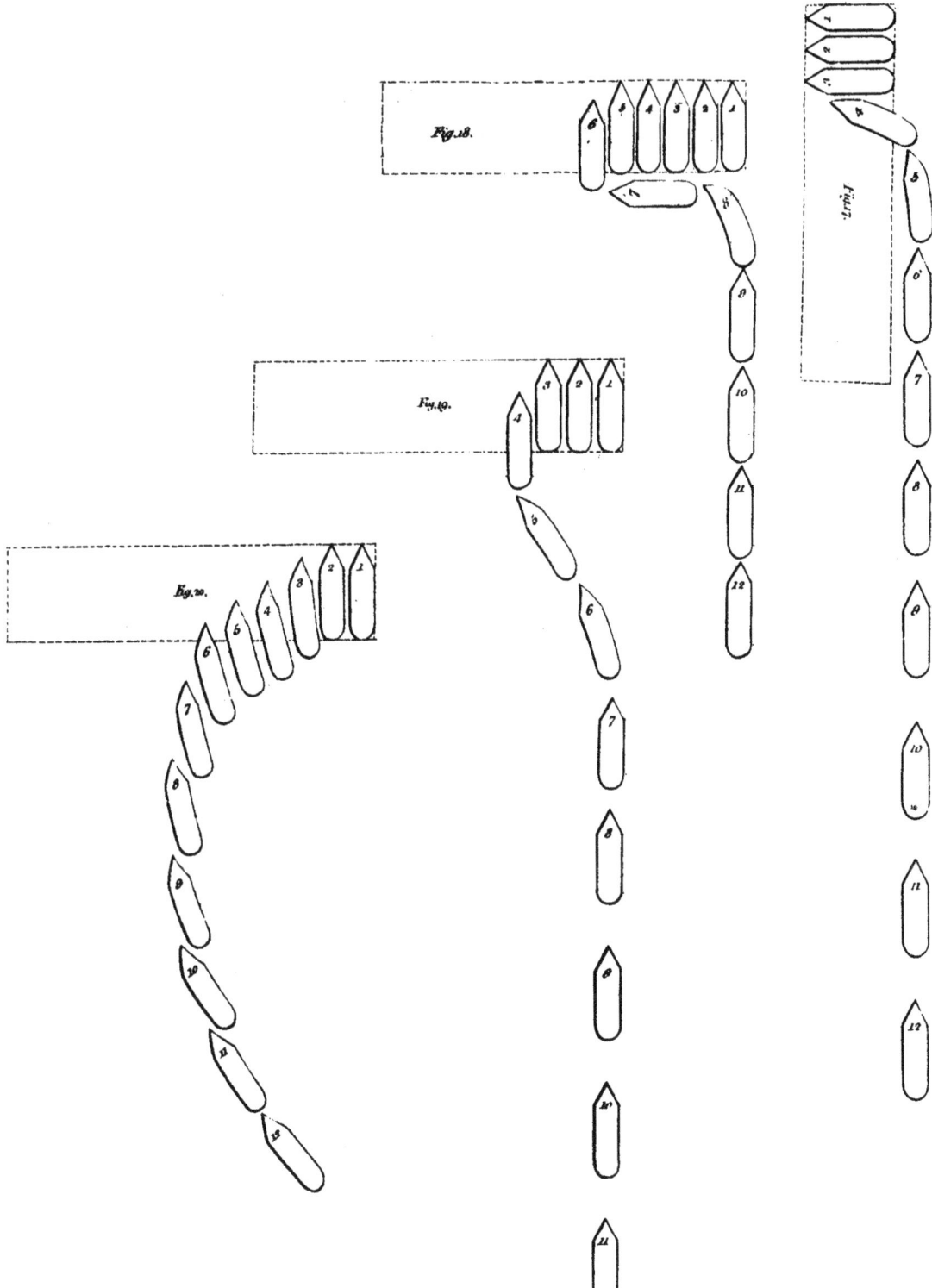

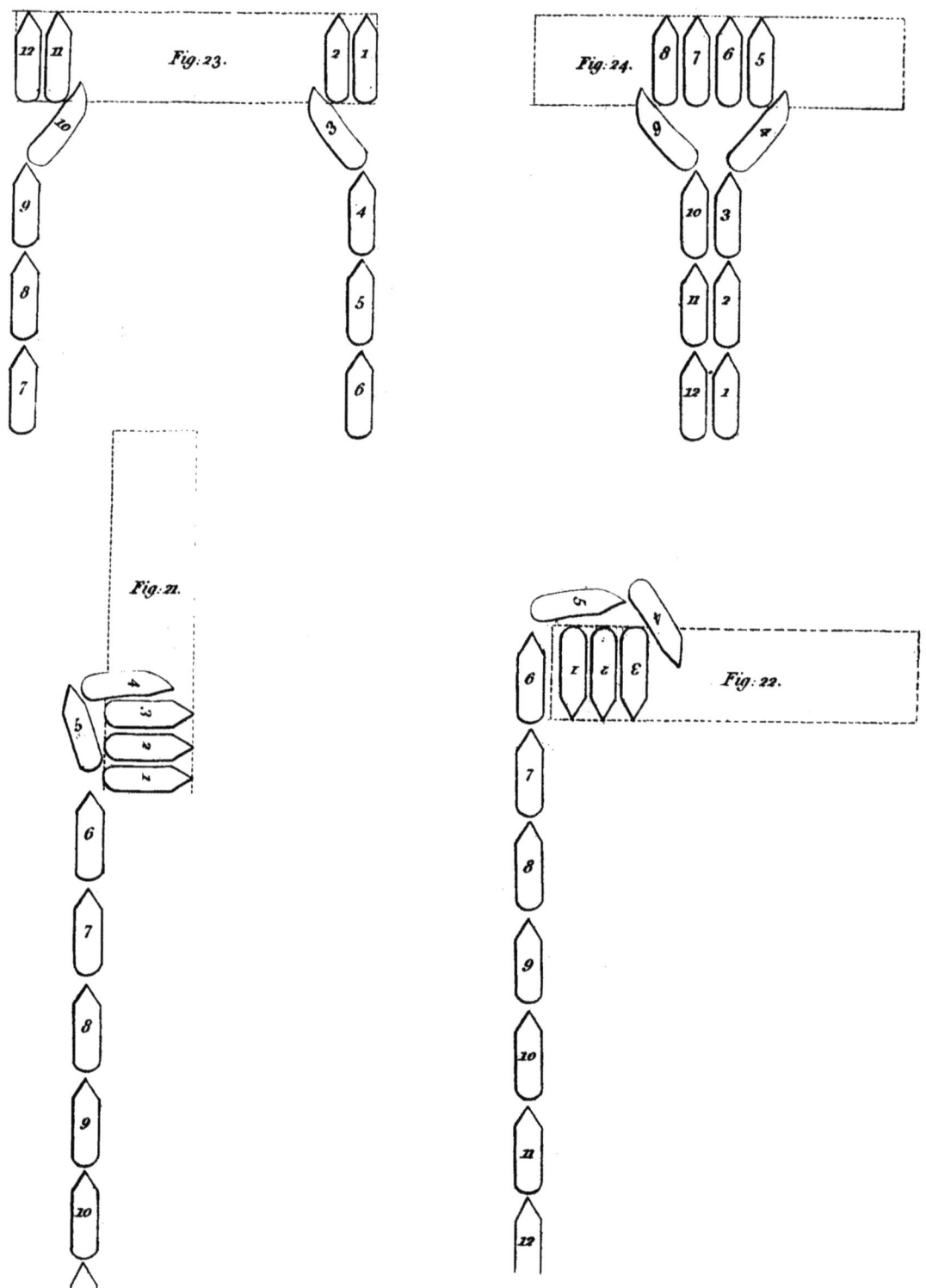

PLATE V.

SECT. XXVI.—*To the Right Form.*

THE leading man faces to the right, the rest keeping close round the croup, form upon him at easy files on the same principle.

[*Fig.* 21.] *Eyes Right.*—Observe strictly to keep close along the croups, and not fly off in a curve.

SECT. XXVII.—*Right About Form.*

The leading man faces to the right about, upon the same principle as before shewn: they form on him at easy files, keeping close round the croup. [*Fig.* 22.]

In this, more than any other mode of forming, men are apt to fly off in a curve, owing to the sharp turns. More care must therefore be taken to avoid this fault. Marching the file nearly up to a wall, and then forming them to the right about, forces them to keep along the croups; if they then fly off to the left, a situation may be chosen where two walls or fences form a right angle—the file marching along under one, and being formed about when arrived near the angle; and thus the men acquire a habit of performing it correctly. They must be careful however not to justle or brush against the croup of other horses, which produces kicking.

Left about form is very seldom used except when filed from the left flank, and then they are seldom form'd to the right about.

It must be observed that when filed from the left flank, every man has to form upon the right hand of his leader, and not upon the left, as in these figures; else their relative situation in the ranks would be changed. It follows that in forming to the left, every man has to pass the man before him, as in Fig. 21, only facing to the left instead of the right, as if that fig. were inverted, though it brings them into the situation of Fig. 17 when formed. On the other hand, when forming to the right, he does not pass round the croup, as in Fig. 21, but only turns up a-breast, as if Fig. 17 were inverted; yet the situation when formed is that of Fig. 21.

So forming to the left *about*, when the left flank is leading, carries them round the croup like the formation of Fig. 22 inverted. It will be understood at once by holding the plates up to the light, seeing through from the other side, and supposing No. 12 leading instead of No. 1.

If the reader is tired with the frequent repetition of the words "*easy files,*" it is hoped it will be impressed on his memory, and never neglected. Crowding in the ranks, not only bruises the knees, but distresses the horses; and in a rapid wheel or charge pressing them out of the line, disturbs the regularity of the movement, and even endangers them by tangling their legs.

Men therefore cannot be too often cautioned to put on the leg in time in forming, and to preserve easy files in the marches, wheels, and charges.

In the REGULATIONS FOR CAVALRY before referred to, it is recommended, that the men and horses be much practised to perform all their manœuvres at *open files*, in order to ensure their performance at *easy files*. It must be remembered that the space of 6 inches is not reckoned between horse and horse, but between *boot-top and boot-top*: which will be more than *eighteen* inches between horse and horse.

SECT. XXVIII.

The troop being in files, from both flanks, as at *Fig.* 15.

Front Form.

The leading men (who are the right and left flank men) halt on the ground, the rest inclining inwards, as they come up to the ground, form within the leading men. [*Fig.* 23.]

SECT. XXIX.

The troop being in files from the centre, [as in *Fig.* 16.]

Front Form.

The two leading men (who are the centre men) halt on the ground, the rest open outward and form: those on the right of the file, on the right, and those on the left, on the left—observing the cautions before laid down. [*Fig.* 24.]

PLATE VI.

Having gone through the various modes of filing and forming, from a single rank, we proceed to the same from two ranks.

SECT. XXX.—*Right File.—March.*

Upon the caution all carry their bridle hands to the right Upon the word " *March*" the rear rank (being at close order, i. e. with the interval of half a horse's length, as before-mentioned), closes up to the croup—The right flank men front and rear wheel to the right and march off a-breast—the rest wait each one in his position, till his turn comes, and then follow; leading and covering files a-breast.   Fig. 25.

> Preserve the intervals in file, as directed in Sect. 17, et seq. The front rank men are always answerable for the intervals, the rear rank men dress by them.

SECT. XXXI.—*From the Right, File to the Front.—March.*

The rear rank closes up, as directed in the last section; the right flank man advances strait forward, his covering file a-breast of him, and on his right. [*Fig.* 26.] The rest file successively to the right, as directed in the last section, till arrived on the ground the first man quitted, when they wheel to the left (i. e. to their original front) and follow the right-hand men as directed in the single filings.

SECT. XXXII.

The same principles followed, in filing TO THE REAR—FROM BOTH FLANKS TO THE FRONT—FROM BOTH FLANKS TO THE REAR—as in the single filings; only the rear rank always first closing up, and leading and covering files moving off a-breast.

> The men should be as much practised to file from the left as from the right flank.

SECT. XXXIII.

From the centre file to the front, is forming columns of fours, and will be explained in another place, except when a squadron is at ORDER or OPEN ORDER, and then they move " BY RANKS" the front rank filing as in Sect. 22, *Fig.* 16, the rear rank following in like manner, as soon as the front is all in file. Eyes right or left, as directed by the officer.

SECT. XXXIV.—*To the Left Form.* [*Fig.* 27.]

Performed exactly as from single rank, [see Sect. 23.] only the leading man advances one and a half horse's length forwarder, to leave room for his covering file to fall behind him at close order.

> No front rank man, must quit the side of his rear rank man, till that rear rank man is just coming into his place; a fault generally committed through hurry. In forming from a double file, the rear rank man, as soon as he is arrived at the croup of the horse on which he is to form, must halt and drop behind his file-leader. In Fig. 27, No. 5, of the rear rank is to halt for that purpose, in the position he is in, till his leading file has pass'd him. So No. 6—in figures 28, 29, 31, and 32.

SECT. XXXV.

It has been observed that forming to the *left about* is seldom used when filed from the right flank: but forming to the right about carries the line of formation to the right of the defile, and it may be wanted on the left. It will be attained by wheeling the file to the left, just the length of the rank, and then forming to the left, as in [*Fig.* 28.] When it is necessary to front the defile, it must be by forming to the left about; which is intricate and difficult. A figure will be given to illustrate it in another place.

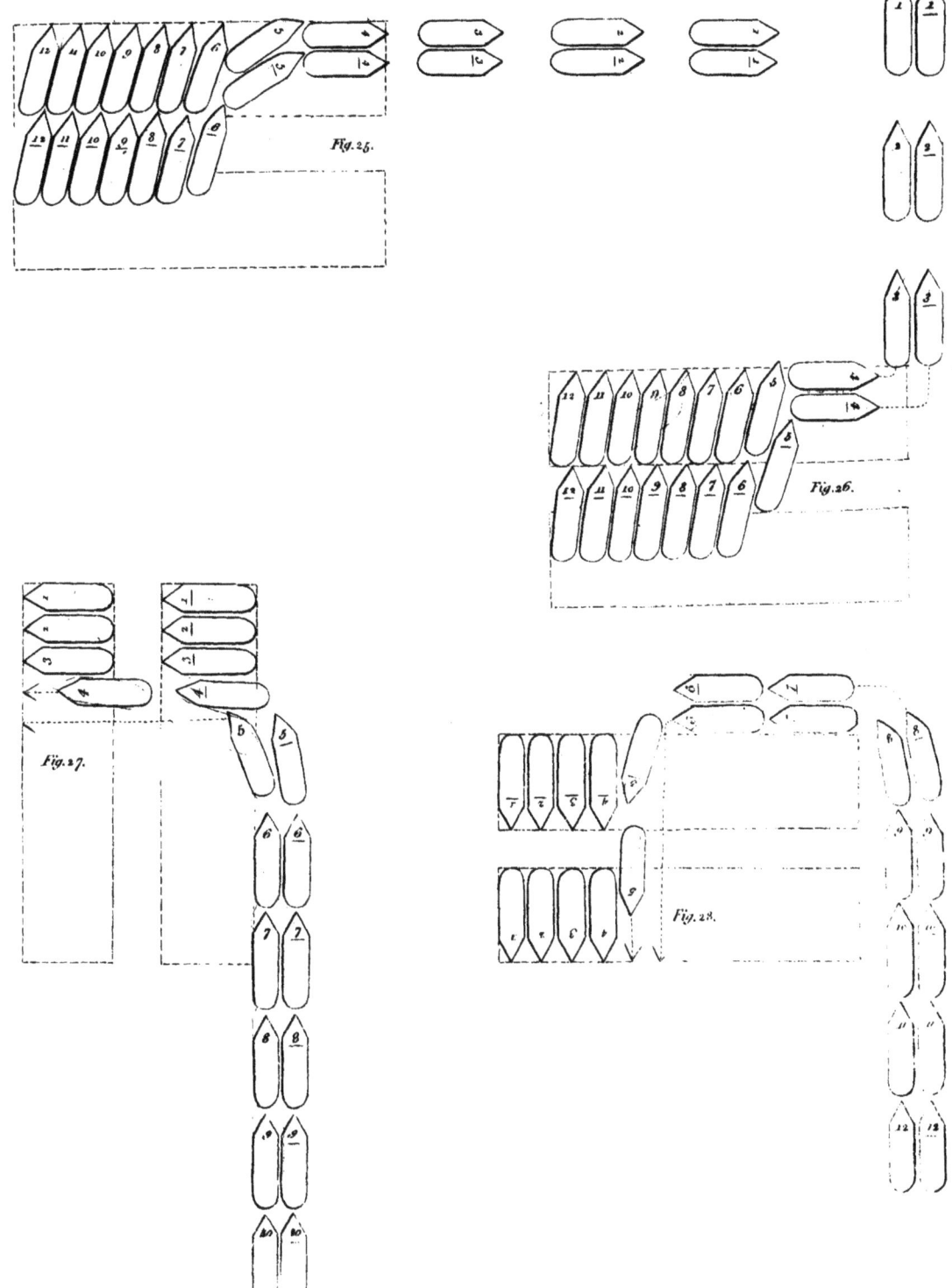

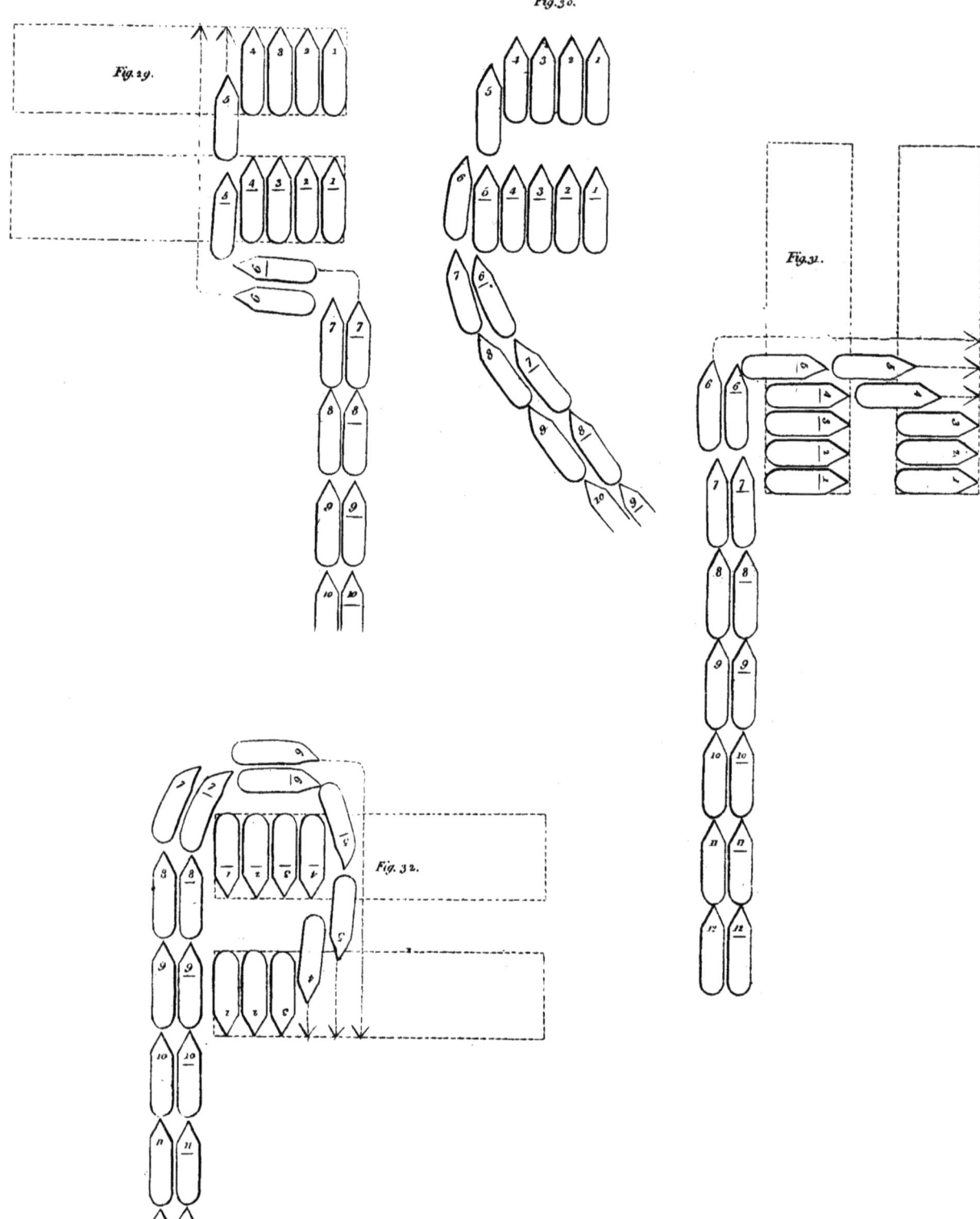

PLATE VII.

SECT. XXXVI.—*To the Front Form.*—[*Fig. 29.*]

See Sect. 24, and observe strictly the caution under Sect. 34.

<small>The faulty manner of performing this, is shewn in Fig. 30, where No. 6, 7, and 8, are seen quitting their covering files, before they are arrived in the lines of formation, contrary to the principles laid down, and the authority before referred to. They must keep a-breast till arrived at the line, when the leading file must move up quickly a-breast of his right-hand man, pulling up however before quite in his place, and putting on his leg in time.</small>

SECT. XXXVII.—*To the Right Form.*—[*Fig. 31.*]

SECT. XXXVIII.—*To the Right about Form.*—[*Fig 32.*]

These figures need no explanation—It is performed in the same manner as when in single rank, (described in sect. 26 and 27. attending to the preceding cautions) except that in forming two ranks, the leading man must advance one and a half horse's length to leave room for the interval of close order, and for the rear rank man.

PLATE VIII.

SECT. XXXIX.—*(Both Ranks being in Files a-breast) By single Files from the Left.*

THE first rear rank man inclines to the left, and drops behind his file leader; the second front rank man slackening his pace sufficiently to make room for him.

The rest do the same when they come up to the same ground. [*Fig.* 33.]

If the left flank leads, the word is, " *by single files from the right,*" the front rank being then on the right hand.

The leading files should in general be ordered into a smart trot; as much time is lost whenever the front is diminished; and on the other hand, to march slow when the front is increased.

In the figure, the files are represented wheeling successively at the angle. The word for which is " leading file! right wheel."

SECT. XL.—*Double up by Twos.—Slow in Front.*

The first rear rank man *inclines to the right and comes a-breast* of his file leader, the second front rank man closes up to his proper interval. The rest do the like as they come up to the same ground. [*Fig.* 34.]

If they were filed originally from the *left flank*, in order to file singly, the rear rank incline to the *right* to drop behind their file leaders, and to the *left* to come again a-breast. [*Fig.* 35.]

The leading files must not be suffered to march fast, as the horses in the rear have so much more ground to go over in doubling up.

A squadron of fifty-six files, when in single files, extends upwards of a quarter of a mile. It is obvious that in doubling up, if the leaders move at the rate of 8 miles an hour, the rear, in order to come into their places in a quarter of a mile, must gallop at the rate of sixteen miles an hour. Some squadrons consist of 80 files.

SECT. XLI.—*Form Threes.*

The rear rank men of the first three drop behind their file leaders, who form a-breast of their right hand man. The others when they come up. [*Fig.* 36.]

This is exactly the same as forming to the front, Sect. 36, *Fig.* 29, only the rank consists of three instead of twelve, and being done on the march, they must come a-breast as early as they can in the manner represented in *Fig.* 30, and there called faulty, because the leaders have halted.

SECT. XLII.—*From the Right of Threes, File to Front.*

All the ranks of threes, front and rear together file successively from the right, leading and covering files a-breast, as in *Fig.* 26. Sect. 31. only being on the march, never go into the horizontal line. [*Fig.* 37.]

From the Left of Threes, File to the Front.

Is used only when marching from the left flank, and is then performed on the same principle as the last, only the left of threes filing off first.

When marching from the *right flank*, there seems to be no advantage in filing from the *left of threes*, and it is objectionable, both because it multiplies unnecessarily the evolutions, and also because the succession of the numbers will be altered thus; viz. 3, 2, 1—6, 5, 4—9, 8, 7—in the same manner as when the ranks go about by threes to the rear, as in *Fig.* 7, Sect. 10.

For the same reason it is *preferable,* when marching from the *left flank.*

In forming threes again from this file, the left of threes continue their march, the centre and right inclining to the *right* to come up a-breast.

SECT. XLIII.—*Threes!—By single Files from the Right.*

The right of threes and his covering file march as they are (only preserving the intervals used in filing). The centre drops behind—his rear rank man covering him, then the left in like manner. [*Fig.* 38.]

Pl. 8.

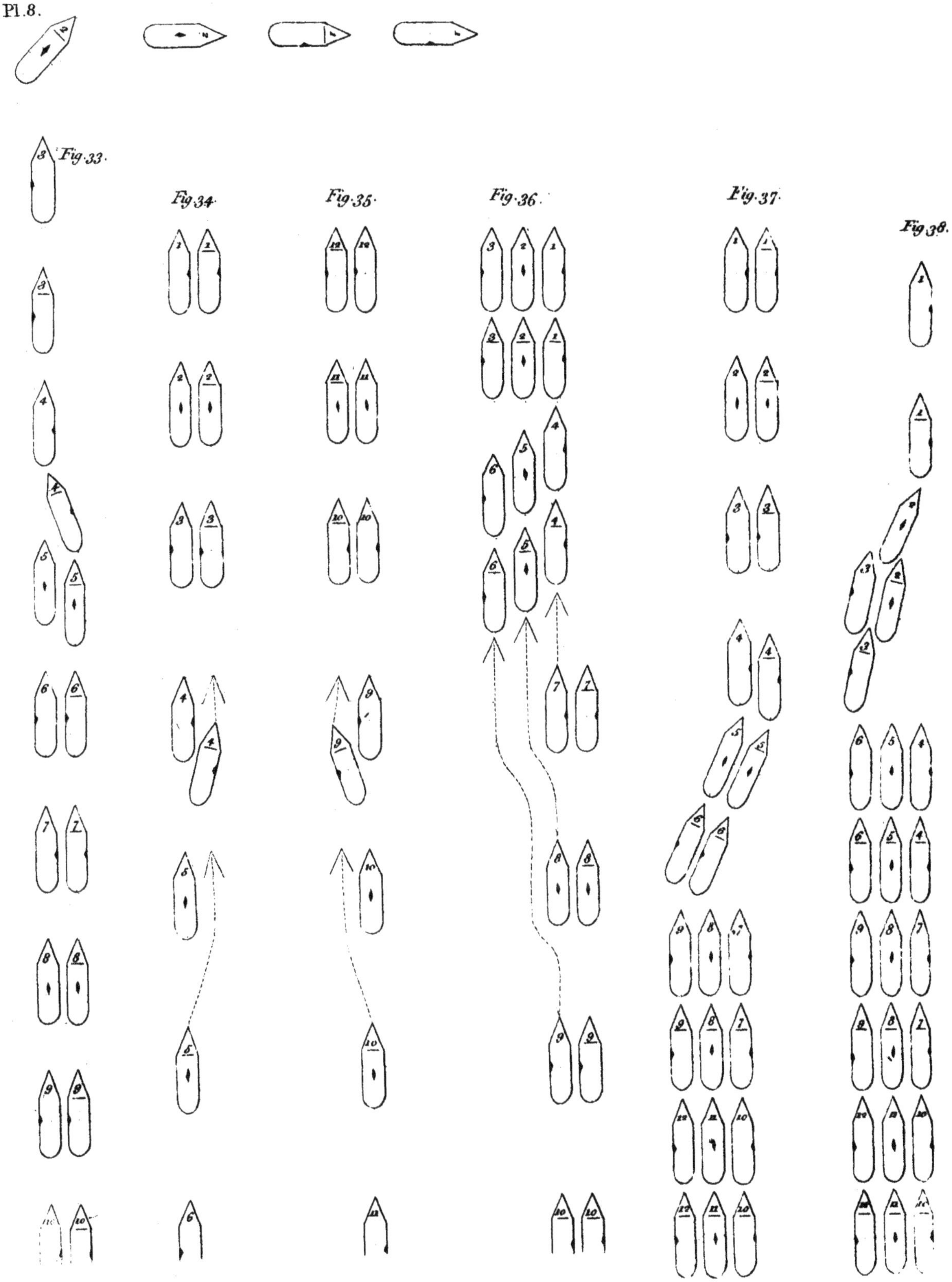

Fig. 33. Fig. 34. Fig. 35. Fig. 36. Fig. 37. Fig. 38.

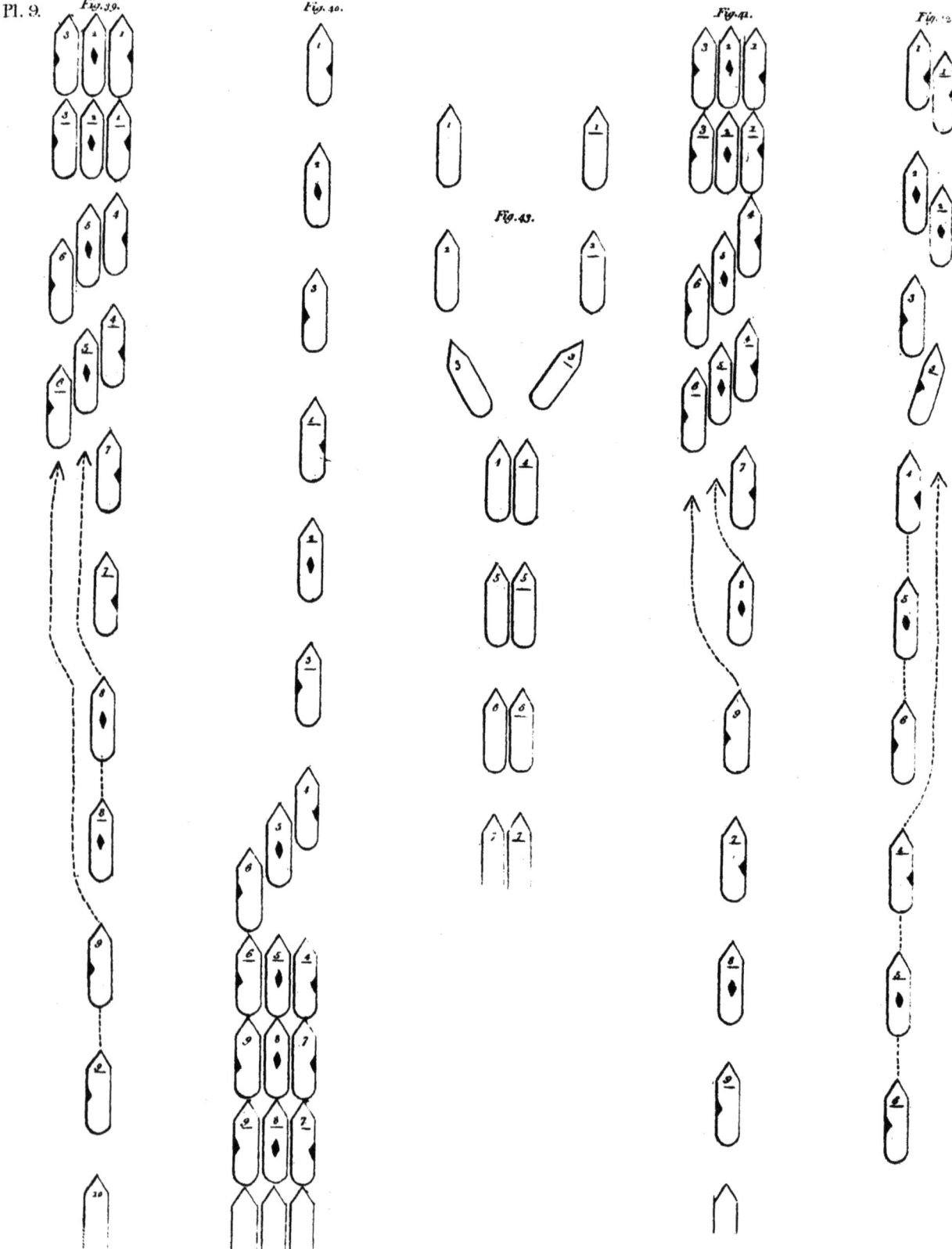

PLATE IX.

SECT. XLIV.—Form Threes (viz. from single Files). [*Note.*]

THE right of threes all move on in the direction they are in. The centre and left men of the *front-rank* threes incline to the left, (each passing the rear-rank man that is before him) and come a-breast of their own right-hand man.

The rear follow and cover. [*Fig. 39, where the dotted lines shew the intended track of the next threes.*]

Note. It is better, in general, (unless they are marching *in a walk*) to double up by twos first, and then form threes; on account of the great distance the rear files have to make up—[*See Note to* Sect. XL.] that proportion increasing in forming threes at once. If they are marching slowly, time will be saved by forming threes at once.

We have now shewn how to diminish the front upon the march from 6 a-breast to 3, 2, or 1, and increase it again as occasion may require.

Simple as these evolutions are when the principle is understood, it is certain that recruits are frequently puzzled in the performance.

The *ranking off of threes* must also be taught. [See *ranking off*, Sect. 15.] It has its advantage, and is, perhaps, a readier and more simple method of diminishing a front of three, and forming again, than the foregoing: but as the preceding is what necessarily follows from double filing, it must be first practised, and become perfectly familiar to the men, before they are taught the following.

SECT. XLV.—Threes! By Ranks—from the Right File to the Front.

The first three of the front rank only file off—then the first three of the rear-rank. The rest as they come up to the ground. [*Fig.* 40.]

Observe the difference between this file and that of **Fig.** 33 and 38.

In *forming threes* from this file the right-hand man marches on in the direction he is in—the centre and left incline to the *left*, and come a-breast of him—first the front rank three, then the rear rank three, and so on alternately as they come up to the same ground.] [*Fig.* 41]

In *doubling up by twos*, all the front-rank men march on in the direction they are in, and all the rear rank incline to the *right*, and come up a-breast of their file-leaders. [*Fig.* 42.]

Each rear-rank man has two to pass before he finds himself a-breast of his file-leader.

If the leading files are from the left flank, the rear rank, in doubling up by twos, inclines to the *left*, as observed in Sect. XL. This occasions no additional difficulty, as the rear rank men cannot but be aware that their file-leaders must be on their right-hand; and it is then better to *rank off* threes from the *left*. [*See Note to* Sect. XLII.]

Recruits always find something intricate in the changing from ranks of threes to files single and double, and *vice versa*. It is, however, precisely the same as the filing and forming of **Fig.** 26 and 29, except that there the ranks consist of 12, here of 3 only. So in ranking off, &c. Let the rear rank men carefully remember their file-leaders, and each one his right and left-hand man. The leading and covering files are never separated in filing or forming. If in single files, they are in file—in double files, they are a-breast—in forming, they are in file again. In *ranking off*, they are separated just the length of the rank.

SECT. XLVI.—Open your Files to the Right and Left. [*Fig.* 43.]

This needs no explanation. It is used where there may be room for the files separated, but not closed: as on both sides of a road where carriages may pass betwixt, or through a wood, across a heath, &c. where the ground is irregular, and a single file can pick its way.

Threes may be opened in like manner.

It has been before observed, that time is always lost in diminishing the front: for which reason, though it will continually be practised at drill by way of rendering it familiar, it will always be avoided on service, when not absolutely necessary. This mode of opening the files in many cases answers the end.

To the Right (or Left) Close your Files,

Brings them as they were.

PLATE X.

The ranks suppofed to be now formed at close order.

SECT. XLVII.—*Rear Rank! Take Sword Exercife-Order.—March.*

The rear rank reins back at leaſt the length of three horses; which leaves room for two horses and three intervals.

SECT. XLVIII.—*Prepare to perform Sword Exercise.*

Upon this *caution* the centre and left of *the right flank threes only*, front and rear, rein back. The centre-man covering exactly his right-hand man, and the left covering him; with the interval of half a horse's length between croup and nofe. [*Fig.* 44.]

All the rest stand fast and wait for the word.

March.

All the other centres and left of threes do the same, dressing by the right and most scrupulously attentive to cover. [*Fig.* 45.]

They are then commanded to prove distances of files, and go through the divisions.

Then to the front form troop or squadron, and then to take close order.

The officer should take care to see that they are at easy files before he gives the word to prepare for Sword Exercise—for if they were previously at close files, there will be barely room for the swords.

Directions for performing Sword Exercise are published by authority, and personal teaching and much practice are necessary.

With respect to performing it *in speed*, (an accomplishment absolutely necessary for a light-horse-man) we may be allowed to make a few remarks.

The necessity of a firm and easy seat, and perfect command of the horse, needs not to be proved; and many positions on the horse are necessary in the sword exercise, which are not used on any other occasion.

The swords-man must sit his horse in full speed with the front of one thigh and even the knee against the saddle, so that his face and sword-arm be directed over the side of the horse towards his antagonist. He must change in an instant in speed to front the opposite side, and also be able to ride looking directly over the horse's croup, with his sword-arm extended over it in the rear cut.

These positions are very different from any taught or used in common riding, and are of themselves difficult. We should therefore recommend, that each poſition, and the quick change from one to another, be separately studied and practised without the sword till perfectly easy and familiar. The best practice is always in a circle: and when the sword is taken up, the divisions must be gone through slowly at first, else the difficulties are multiplied one into another—bad habits are got and fixt—and perhaps the horse struck and rendered for ever unsteady.

With respect to one part of this exercise, viz. the giving point to infantry, it is remarked by Colonel Tyndale (Mil. Equit. p. 55.) that false principles of riding are introduced; such as, leaning forward, abandoning the horse and urging him forward without a perfect command over him, to the very great danger of the rider: and we are informed in the same passage, that Colonel Le Marchant (to whom the army is indebted for this useful exercise) disapproves and disclaims the practice. To which remark we may add, that although a man may find it easy to exhibit this on smooth ground, thrusting the point of his sword into the earth while his horse gallops right forward, yet when he comes to put it in practice against an enemy, his horse leaping over or trampling on men lying under him, or starting to avoid the thrust of a bayonet, he may find too late the ill effects of ever quitting a firm position in the saddle, or trusting his safety to his horse's good will.

We must also recommend, that when the men are drawn up in divisions for the purpose of going through the sword exercise in speed, whether they are to perform it two at a time, or four at a time, they should all ride from the same end. If there are only two divisions drawn up for the purpose, (one on each flank of the regiment or squadron) two men may ride from the same division, viz. one from each flank. Then two from the opposite division in like manner. So if there are four divisions (two on each flank) four may ride in like manner from one end, and then four from the opposite end. Horses are less likely to swerve, when galloping the same way, than when passing each other. If they do, the consequences are less mischievous: and it is (probably for this reason) now become the most usual practice in the army to ride, as here recommended, from the same end. It has this advantage also, viz. that the officer can see both or all the swords-men at the same time, which he cannot do when coming from opposite points.

Gentlemen must also make it a serious rule, to slope swords immediately upon any effort of the horse to quit his ground; and by no means continue the division when the horse swerves.

Upon the whole, the sword exercise, in real speed, should not be too often practised. It is certainly distressing to the horses—a matter now of national importance. It is not necessary—for though a man, who can perform the sword exercise in line with tolerable accuracy, finds a new difficulty from the motion of the horse, (particularly in the sway it creates in the arm in the aſſault) yet, when he can perform it correctly in a canter, he finds little or no additional difficulty in the swiftest gallop, except that he has (in the same space of ground) less time for the division: for which reason, when practising in a slow gallop, he should perform it in shorter lengths.

Pl. 10.

Fig. 45.

Fig. 44.

Fig. 46.

SECT. XLIX.—*Prepare to Dismount.*

They close files to the right. [Note.] Then if the troop is at ORDER, the left files of both ranks, (the files being previously told off alternately right and left) rein back one horse's length, dressing by the right and covering the intervals. [*Fig.* 46.]

They are then at *open files*. [See Sect. I.]

[Note—*Close files*.] For explanation see Sect. I. They are closed for the sake of linking the horses.

If they are at CLOSE ORDER, the right files of the front rank advance one horse's length, and the left files of the rear rank rein back, [*Fig.* 46] putting a lock of the mane into the bridle-hand. Then by signal from a fleugel-man, placed for the purpose considerably in front and on the right flank, they stoop and bring up the right stirrup over the horse's shoulder.

Dismount.

They dismount, lay the left stirrup over the horse's shoulder, and face themselves to the front, holding the rein in the right hand near the bit.

They may be ordered to stand at ease, or to lead the horses into line.

If ordered to link the horses, the files that reined back lead the horses into line; face on foot to the right about—undo the collars—give each the end of his collar-strap to his right-hand man (now standing on his left) who puts the end through the ring of his own collar, and passes it to the next on his left, who fastens it to the ring. The motions of the individuals of course are successive; for a man cannot take on his right and give on his left at the same time; and as the right-flank-man has to take only (for he alone should not unfasten his collar-strap) they begin from his left-hand man; who first with his left hand gives his collar-strap, then with his right takes his left-hand man's, and puts it through his ring—with his left hand again passes it to his neighbour—then with his right hand, takes another collar from his left-hand man, and fastens it to his own ring. The length between the horses' heads, should be about 18 inches. If much shorter, the horses' heads are brought too near, and their croups thrown out, forming a curve instead of a right line. If much longer, the horses are too much at liberty, and some will hang back or thrust themselves forward, disordering the rank. This being done, each man faces to the right about to front.

If marched off, the front-rank march forwards closing to the centre, and halt. The rear-rank men file outwards from both flanks, wheel by files to the front to pass the horses, and form to the front, behind the front-rank men, the flank file of every division being left with the horses; as are the quarter-master and farriers.

In unlinking, the same regularity must be observed, and the collar-straps fastened to the saddles; taking care to pass them under the rein to clear them, and to leave room for the play of the horses' heads; but no spare length of collar hanging down, in danger of tangling with the accoutrements of the neighbour. In the regulars, they undo the collar-straps before dismounting, and afterwards mount before they fasten them up. But as the horses of volunteer corps are not generally so steady as those of the army, it may be better for them to practice as here directed.

SECT. L.—*Prepare to Mount.*

If they are in line they lead the horses back (or forward as the case may be) into the position of Fig. 46, bring the stirrup from the shoulder and wait for the word MOUNT, to be obeyed by all in one instant, pausing first in the stirrup, then the leg thrown over and the horses brought into line—all the motions exactly from the fleugel-man.

Frequent mounting and dismounting with the regular pauses, steadies the horses very much. Gentlemen should never allow a horse (when mounting for the road) to move till they are in the seat, and after a pause of a moment give him the signal. If they will sometimes employ a few minutes in mounting and dismounting, they will find it good exercise, and time spent not unprofitably either to man or horse.

PLATE XI.

THE interval between horses in rank, called *double distance* (see Sect 1.) is the proper position for performing the manual exercise with pistols on horseback.

There are several ways of bringing the troop to *double distance*. One is shewn in Sect. 48.—but six horses in file make too long a line for the manual exercise, as the rear is too much out of sight of the officer. They may form rank entire by advancing by single files from the right or left, or by ranking off outwards from both flanks, close to the croup, and when all in file wheel (each on his own ground) to the front; but if the squadron is numerous, the rank by these means becomes too much extended. The best way seems to be to advance the right of threes, let them go through the exercise, retire to their places, and then advance the centre men of threes, and afterwards the left in like manner. The ranks may be opened to a sufficient interval that both ranks may have room to perform it at the same time, or they may form a rank entire of threes alternately front and rear, as follows:

SECT. LI.—Threes!—Right Wheel—March.

They wheel as in Sect. 6, Fig. 5.

Forwards—March.

Rear Rank! left incline and cover.

[See Sect. XV. *Fig.* 10.]

Halt—Threes! wheel up—March. Halt—Right Dress.

They will now be in the position of Fig. 47.

From rank entire thus formed they may rein back to the sword-exercise position, three deep instead of six, and perform the manual exercise all together. Or,

SECT LII.—The Right of Threes will advance for Manual Exercise—March.

The right of threes advance about three horses' length, halt, and dress by the right. The centres and left stand fast. [*Fig.* 48.]

If they were in two ranks and at open order, the right of the rear-rank threes advance to half the distance between the ranks.

MANUAL EXERCISE.

Prepare to perform Manual Exercise.

They take off the right-hand gloves—loofe the pistol-holsters and cartouch-box.

Load your Left Pistol.

They draw it with the right hand, (over the reins) place it in the left (which also holds the reins) nearly horizontally, but rather pointing upwards and a little to the left—open the pan—draw the cartridge—bite off the end—shake a little powder into the pan and shut it—the first finger and thumb still holding the cartridge, the second finger crossing over the butt assists in casting the pistol round so as to bring the muzzle upwards, the guard inwards next the body, and the butt against the left side of the stomach—load—ram the cartridge gently down (first taking care that all the powder shakes out, into the barrel)—return ramrod—grasp the pistol in the right hand below the guard, and bring it to the right side of the stomach, the cock against the breast, the muzzle still pointing up and a little forward. At the word

Make Ready,

Grasp it again in the left hand, cock with the right, and bring it back to the last-mentioned position.

It is sometimes practised to carry it on the holster, but it is not so carried in the army, and it is a very objectionable mode.

To the Front, Present.

The pistol is raised and pointed to the front—on a level with the eye—the left eye shut, and the right eye taking aim along the barrel of the pistol.

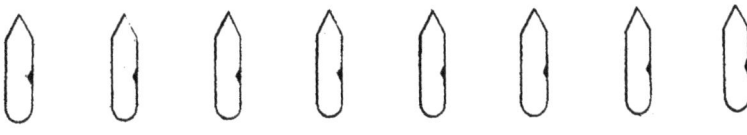

Fire.

Immediately on firing, the pistol is to be returned (over the reins) into the holster.

Draw Swords.

Return Swords.

Load.

Motions as before, only the trigger having been pulled they will have to half cock instead of opening the pans. After loading, the pistol brought to the right side and pointing upward as before.

Left Face.—March.

Each faces to the left on his own ground.

Make Ready.

Right Present.

The pistol raised and pointed to the right, and aim taken as before.

Fire.

They fire and return pistols as before.

Draw Swords.

Wheel up.

Each faces up to the front.

Return Swords.—Load.

Right Face.—Make Ready.

Left Present.—Fire.

Pistols returned.

Draw Swords.

Wheel up.

Return Swords.

The motions may be upon signal from the fleugel instead of word of command, except the facing, which should be by word of command.

They resume their places in the ranks either by facing to the right about, or by reining back as may be ordered; and the centres, and afterwards the left of threes advance in like manner, go through the exercise, and resume their places in rank, [as at *Fig.* 47.]

The use of the pistol should be taught on foot, before it is attempted on horseback. For, simple as the motions are, every thing is awkwardly done that is not regularly practised and become habitual: and in this particular, awkwardness is dangerous.

It will also be right to practice at a target, with ball-cartridges; but this must not be allowed to any one who has not previously shewn himself thoroughly handy in the business with powder only. With ball cartridges they must advance successively, from a rank regularly drawn up, and fire singly; and not the smallest deviation from the regular minutiæ of the motions, ever pass unnoticed by the officer. No man must quit his place on any account, or make any motion with his pistol after it is loaded and before his turn to advance and fire. After firing, he must retreat, and come round by the rear to the reverse flank, and there load. If a pistol misses fire the soldier must recollect, that for fire-arms to go off sometime after the trigger is pulled, is a common occurrence; and he must expect it, and point his pistol upright, that the ball may fly harmless in the air. Any want of seriousness, attention, or regularity, may prove fatal.

When the firing is ceased, the men must remain in rank, and every pistol be tried singly with the ramrod, under the eye of the officer or serjeant, that if any have missed fire, they may be fired or drawn.

The ball-cartridges will of course be delivered in a certain number to each man, and every cartouch-box afterwards examined by the serjeant appointed for that purpose.

SECT. LIII.—*Rear Rank! Rein Back.—March.*

The rear rank threes rein back to close order. [*Fig.* 49.] They may then cover to the right either by passaging, filing and forming, or wheeling by threes to the right, closing up to the croup and wheeling up.

[*Fig.* 50.] Represents a troop in file countermarching to the right about, and will be referred to in a subsequent section.

PLATE XII.

The intention of this plate is, to point out the manner in which the standard with his covering serjeant is to find his place, when threes are wheeled to the right or right about. The tellings off of a squadron, and the position of the squadron and flank officers, &c. will be afterwards shewn. For the present it is sufficient to say that the officer bearing the standard takes his post in the centre; a serjeant covers him, and they are not told in with the threes. The former is distinguished in the plate by a flag, the latter by the letter S. [See *Fig.* 51.] The figures include only the two centre threes of the squadron front and rear. The right and left men of half squadrons are distinguished by an additional outer line on the half diamond.

SECT. LV.

When threes wheel to the right or left, the standard is to march between the front and rear rank, in rank with the rear threes of the leading half squadron: his covering-serjeant behind him in rank with the leading threes of the rear half squadron, as in [*Fig.* 53, and 58.] For this purpose, when wheeling to the right, the standard must wheel back with the right flank man of the left half squadron as far as a half wheel—when perceiving that he has cleared the croup of the three on his right, he instantly pushes on to his place in the direction of the dotted line. [*Fig.* 52.]

During this time the covering serjeant moves forward with the left flank man of the right half squadron just half the wheel, and then reins back into his place behind the standard. They are then in the situation of [*Fig.* 53.]

When they wheel up, the standard first slips back along the same dotted line, and then comes up a-breast of the man with whom he before wheeled back—The serjeant pushes forward to come a-breast of the left flank man of the right half squadron, and then reins back with him.

When wheeling by threes to the left, the motion is inverted and will be seen by holding the plate up to the light, and seeing from the reverse side.

SECT. LVI.

When wheeled to the right about, the standard and his covering file remain each on his own ground, but faced to the rear. As they have not room to turn on their own ground, the serjeant should rein back with the right of the three on his left, as far as the half wheel, as at Fig. 54, then push forwards nearly a-breast of the right of the three on his right, as at Fig. 55, with whom he wheels back, as at Fig. 56, into his place, Fig. 57.

The standard officer might face about in the same way, but if the ranks are too close, or the horses not handy, his motion in front is easier than between the ranks. He moves out in front, inclining to the left, faces to the right, and comes round with the left of the three on his left; Figs. 54, 55, 56, and 57.

SECT. LVII.

When, after wheeling by threes to the right, as in [*Fig.* 53.] the column is countermarched by wheeling by threes to the right about, the standard and his covering file have to change places, as well as to face about.

It is by no means difficult if done regularly. The standard wheels backwards with the right of threes then on his left; the serjeant wheels forwards with the left of three on his right, and when half the wheel-about is complete, they will be in the situation of [*Fig.* 57.] Then the standard wheels forward with the left of the three on his right, and the serjeant backwards with the right of the three on his left.

If in a flank march the left flank leading, they are in like manner countermarched, the motion is exactly the same as last above directed. (For "threes about" is always *right* about). The standard wheels backward, the serjeant forwards, and they will (on the half-wheel-about) find themselves, the former in the rear rank, the latter in the front rank; then the standard wheeling forwards and the serjeant backwards they are in their places, as in [*Fig.* 53.]

These evolutions are well worth practising, and involve the duty not only of the cornet but of the privates; for the motion of the threes on his right and left must coincide with his.

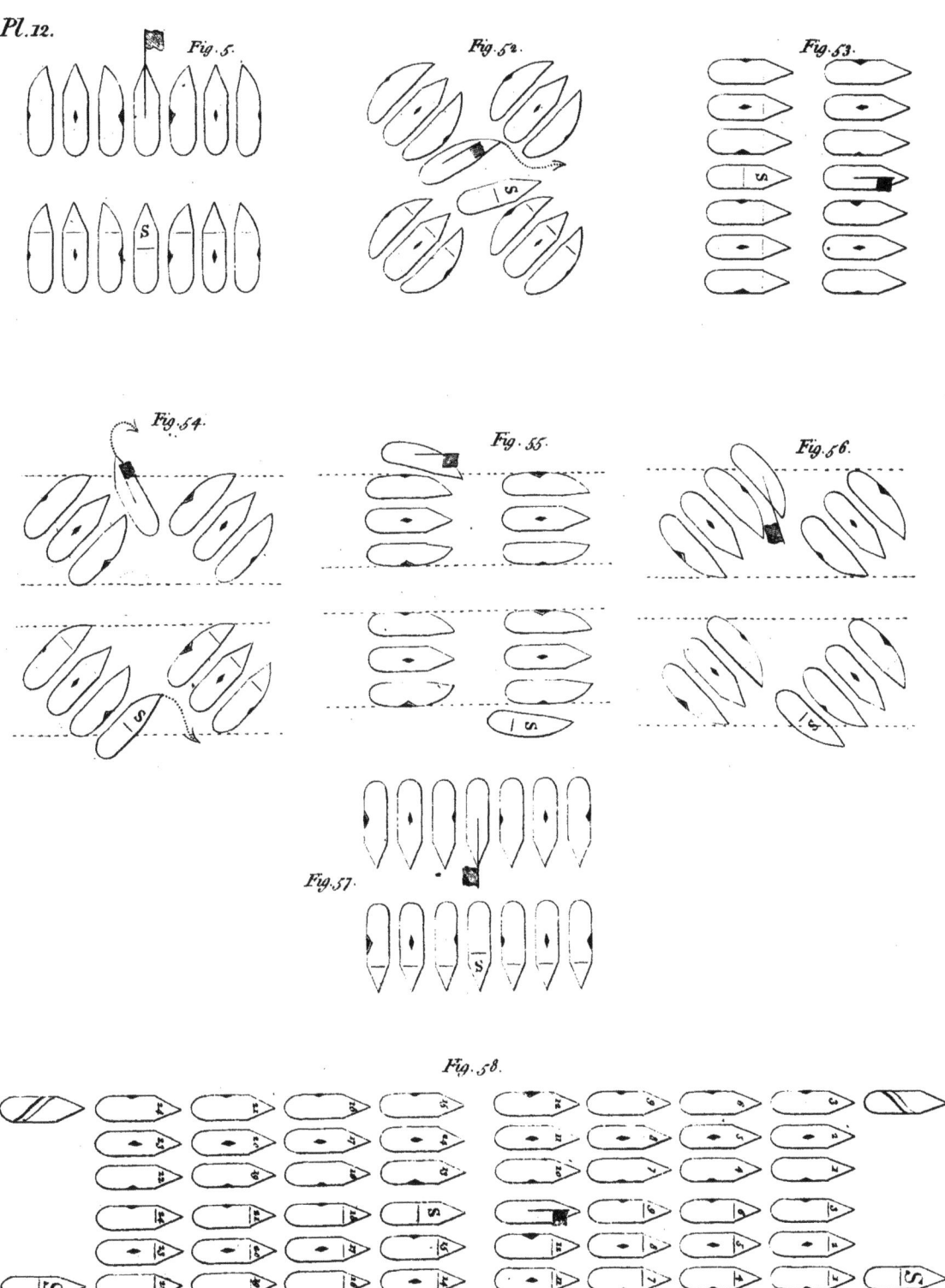

Pl.13.

Fig. 59.

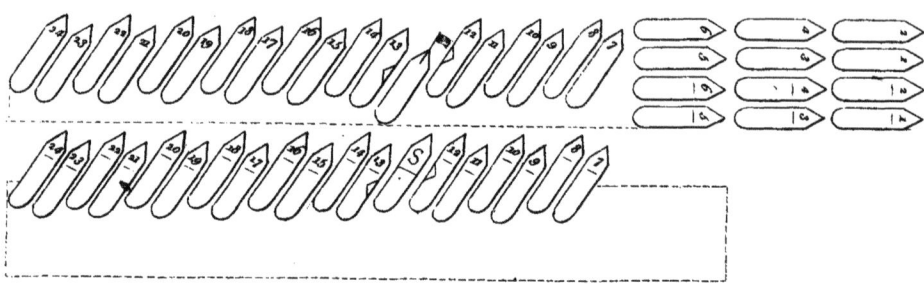

Fig. 60.

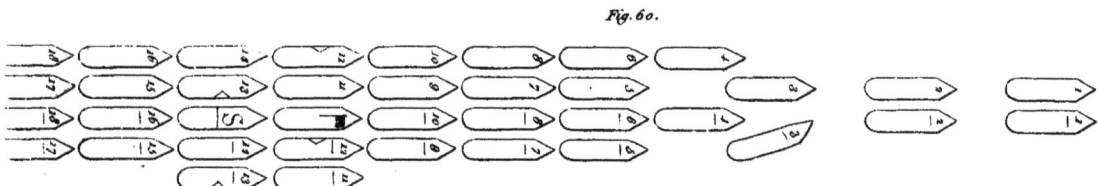

Fig. 61.

Fig. 63.

Fig. 62.

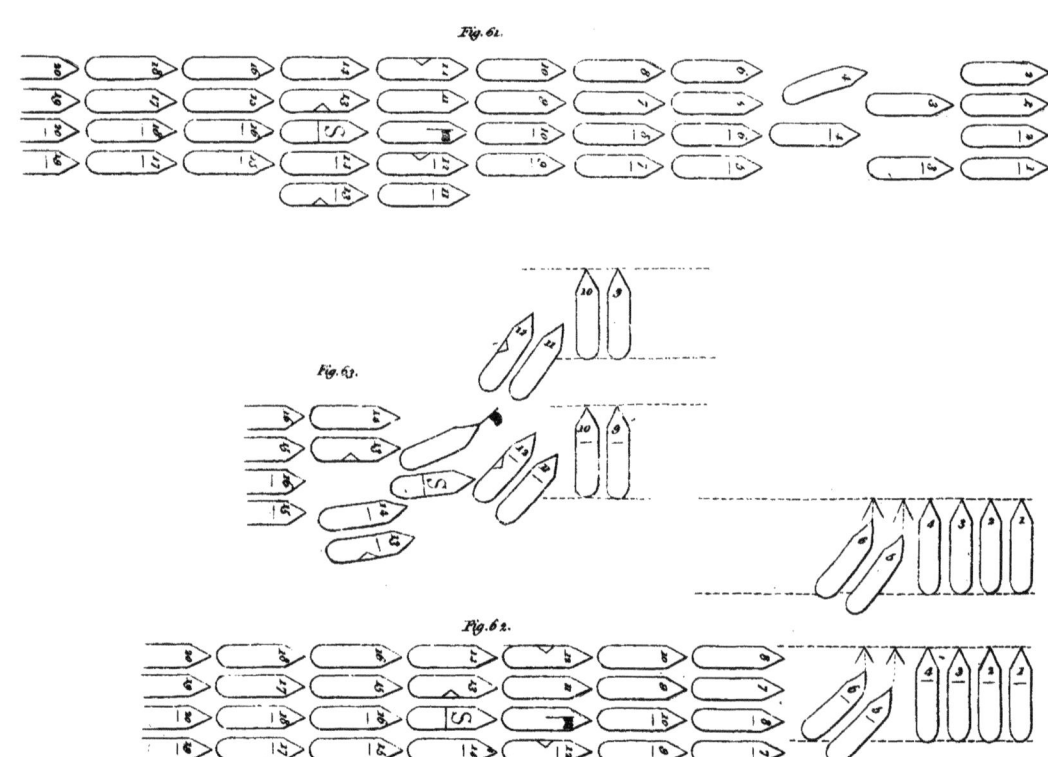

SECT. LVIII.

When wheeled by threes to the right or left, into a column of sixes, the ranks in which the standard and his covering file are, will consist of seven. The rear rank threes a-breast of them must quit those whom they would otherwise cover, and out-flank on the reverse side, [see *Fig.* 58.] In this position if the threes have wheeled correctly, there will be a space between the half squadrons (as in *Fig.* 58.) this space is usually closed in upon, but there are two reasons why it ought not to be. First, the whole rear half squadron of the column must move to fill it up; whereas they ought to remain halted firm, and dressed without ever quitting their ground: and secondly, because on wheeling up, the space is wanted for the standard and serjeant. If this space is not left, they have to crowd themselves in by force, and the space of easy files so material to the ease and regularity of the rank is lost. If indeed they were previously at close files, (which too often happens from inattention) it is impossible for the standard officer to get into his place at all, till the whole squadron has moved to make room for him.

PLATE XIII.

SECT. LIX.—*Ranks by Twos! Right Wheel.*

Upon the caution, the right files wheel as much as they can on the horses' fore legs. The left files advancing one pace to keep exactly a-breast of them. The rear rank closes up and wheels in the same degree.

March.

As there is not room for twos to wheel like threes on their own ground, this can only be done in succession, beginning at the flank, which, on the word, is to wheel to the right and move on in a walk. [See *Fig.* 59.]

> Dress by the left, which is the pivot flank. The standard wheels half backwards with the right of the two on his left, and then pushes forwards. The covering serjeant wheels half forwards with the left of the two on his right, and then suffers the standard to pass him: just as when wheeled by threes in [Sect. LV.] only as the twos continue to march forwards, the serjeant has no occasion to rein back. They march between the front and rear rank, as in [*Fig.* 60 *and* 61.]

SECT. LX.—*Ranks by Twos! from the Right File to the Front.*

The right of twos, front and rear, continue their march, the rear rank men inclining to come a-breast of their file leader. The left of twos drop behind them as in [*Fig.* 60.] The cornet drops behind, and his serjeant comes a-breast of him, marching between the half squadrons.

> It is not expedient to diminish the front by inclining and covering, as in threes; because if they should then wheel up into rank entire, it would put them in a new situation and create confusion.

SECT. LXI.—*Form Ranks by Twos.*

The left of the front rank twos incline to the left, and come a-breast of their right-hand men. The right of the rear rank twos incline to the right to leave room for their left men, who push into the space left for them. [See *Fig.* 61.]

To be done in succession as they come up to ground where the leaders are when the word is given.

SECT. LXII.—*Twos! Left Wheel and Form.*

The leading twos of the column wheel up, the front advancing one and a half horses' length; the rest wheel up and form in succession [as in *Fig.* 62.]

The standard of course does not wheel up with the two on his left, as it would bring him out of his place in the centre. He must drop behind to come a-breast of the right flank man of the left half squadron: the covering serjeant at the same time pushing forward, they wheel up singly into their own places in the centre. [*Fig.* 63.]

SECT. LXIII.

A squadron is sometimes told off in fours. It seems unnecessary to give any description of wheeling by fours, it being so nearly similar to that of threes. They turn altogether upon an imaginary centre between the two centre men.

PLATE XIV.

SECT. LXIV. From the Centre, Form Column of Fours to the Front.

Upon the caution, the standard with his coverer, and the four centre men front and rear, advance sufficiently to clear the front rank [*Fig.* 64.] and, upon the word

March.

The right half squadron files from the left, the left half squadron from the right, to the front, and march forwards following the centre men close to the croup, (*Note*) as in [*Fig.* 65.] The leaders dress by the centre; the rest must all cover regularly, the rear rank men dressing by the front, and the space behind the standard and his covering serjeant will be left open throughout the column.

> The column of fours to the front is sometimes formed by advancing only the standard and covering serjeant and the *two* centre men, upon the caution; the latter opening outwards to admit their covering files, and then the rest follow, filing as above mentioned: but the mode directed in this section is preferable.
>
> (*Close to the Croup.*) It has been before mentioned, that these words do not signify that they are to *touch*, for that must be carefully avoided.
>
> For the method of *wheeling* see afterwards plate 17.

SECT. LXV. To the Front Form Squadron.

Represented in [*Fig* 66.]

SECT. LXVI. To the Right Form Squadron.

Represented in [*Fig.* 67.] The leading fours, with the standard and covering serjeant, wheel to the right upon the right flank man, and the rest form on them.

After the instructions for filing and forming, in former pages, these figures need no explanation.

> In [*Fig.* 66.] the men must continue in column close up to the centre of the rear rank, and not diverge from the column towards the flanks, which they are very apt to do.

In [*Fig.* 67.] the left half squadron are represented inclining to the right, in order to keep close along the croups of those already in rank; which must not be neglected. They are to pass the right half squadron of course; but the front rank men must never quit their covering files, till arrived at the croup of those already formed, when the rear rank man must halt to let his leader pass him. No. 4. and No. 21. in [*Fig.* 66.] and No. 6. and 18. in [*Fig.* 67.] are in this situation.

> These remarks are made in the preceding directions for forming from the march in file, to which the reader is referred. It is hoped this repetition will be excused, for the plainest matters must be frequently repeated when there is an universal tendency to deviate from the regular mode. In these formations there are five faults generally committed, viz.
>
> First, when men attempt from hurry to come a-breast of the man before them instead of following him in file, as if No. 1, 2, and 3, (Front rank men) in [*Fig.* 66.] were pushing on a-breast of No. 4. (See *Fig.* 20. and the observations on it Sect. 25.)
>
> Secondly, when a front rank man quits his covering file before he is arrived at the spot where he is to form; as if in [*Fig.* 66.] No. 3. and No 22. (front rank men) should push on to the vacant place before them. This is an absurd impatience. If those behind them follow this example, all have lost their covering files and are in confusion, (as in *Fig.* 30. *Sect.* 36.) if not there is a vacant space behind them instead of before them, and of course no time is gained.
>
> A third fault is, going off from the direct line of the file diagonally towards the flanks, instead of keeping in a right line up close to the rear rank formed.
>
> A fourth is, when the rear rank man does not halt to let his leader pass—as if the rear rank men, No. 4 and 21, in [*Fig.* 66.] and No. 6 and 18, in [*Fig.* 67.] should push into their places, and throw off their file leaders into a curve.
>
> A fifth is, when the whole loosen out to the flanks in curves, instead of turning at regular angles: to which we may add, crowding against the man on whom they form, and overshooting so as to be under the necessity of reining back. They ought to put on the leg in time, in order to keep the files duly open, and halt before quite in their places (as directed in *Sect.* 23 and notes) so as to move up slowly the last step. Much more than the time apparently lost in care of this sort, will be saved in dressing.
>
> The best general remedy where faults of this nature prevail, will be for the officer at drills to halt them in the midst of the evolution, (as in the present instance, while part are in file, and part formed), and then see that every man is in his proper line of direction.

SECT. LXVII. To the Left Form.

Forming to the left, is precisely the same as to the right, only inverted.

> From a column of fours the squadron may easily be formed with any degree of obliquity to the column, by means of the head of the column wheeling in any degree ordered; as a half, quarter or eighth wheel.

Forming to the right about, is shewn [*Plate* 16. *Fig.* 74]

Pl.14.

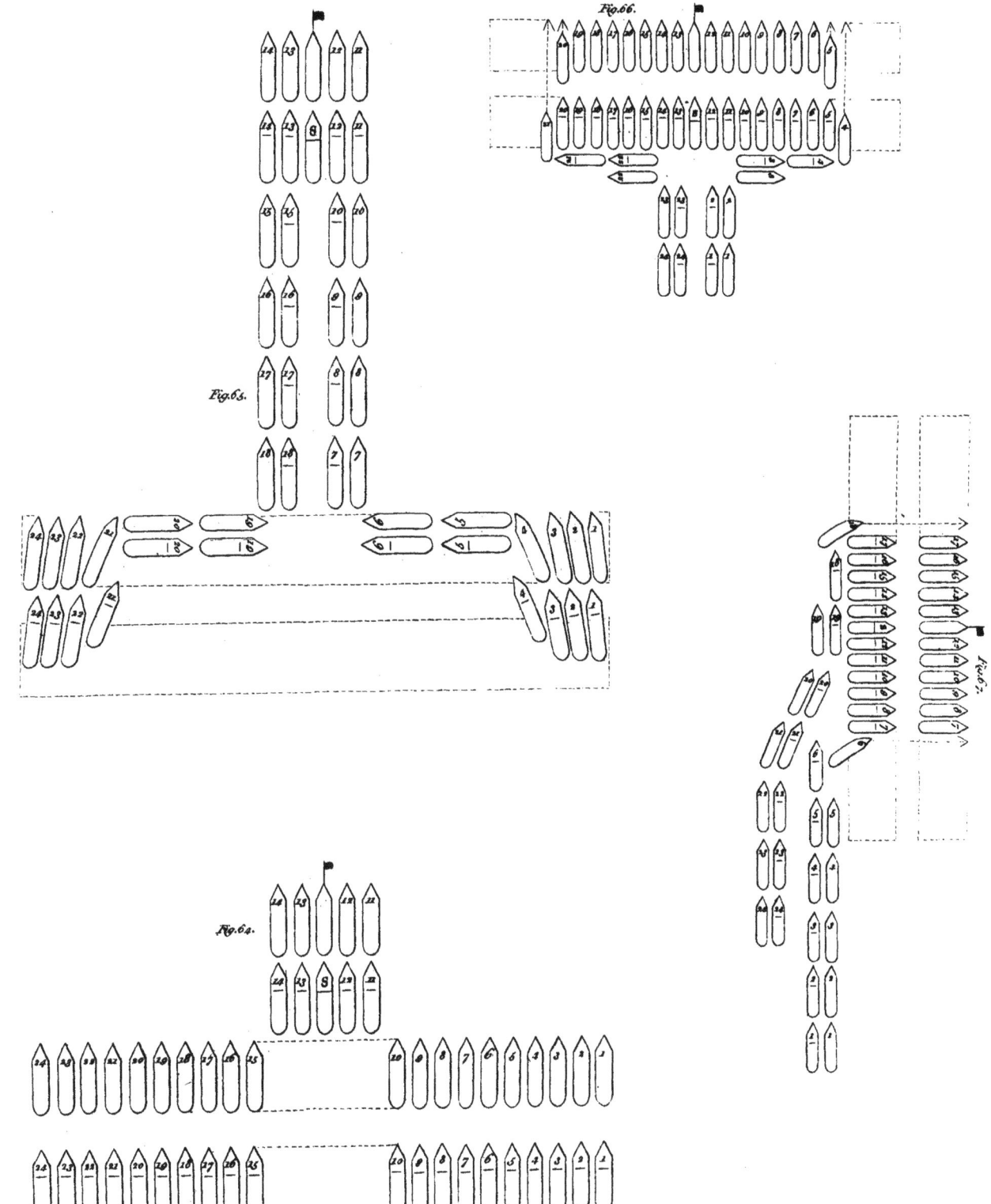

Fig.65.

Fig.66.

Fig.67.

Fig.64.

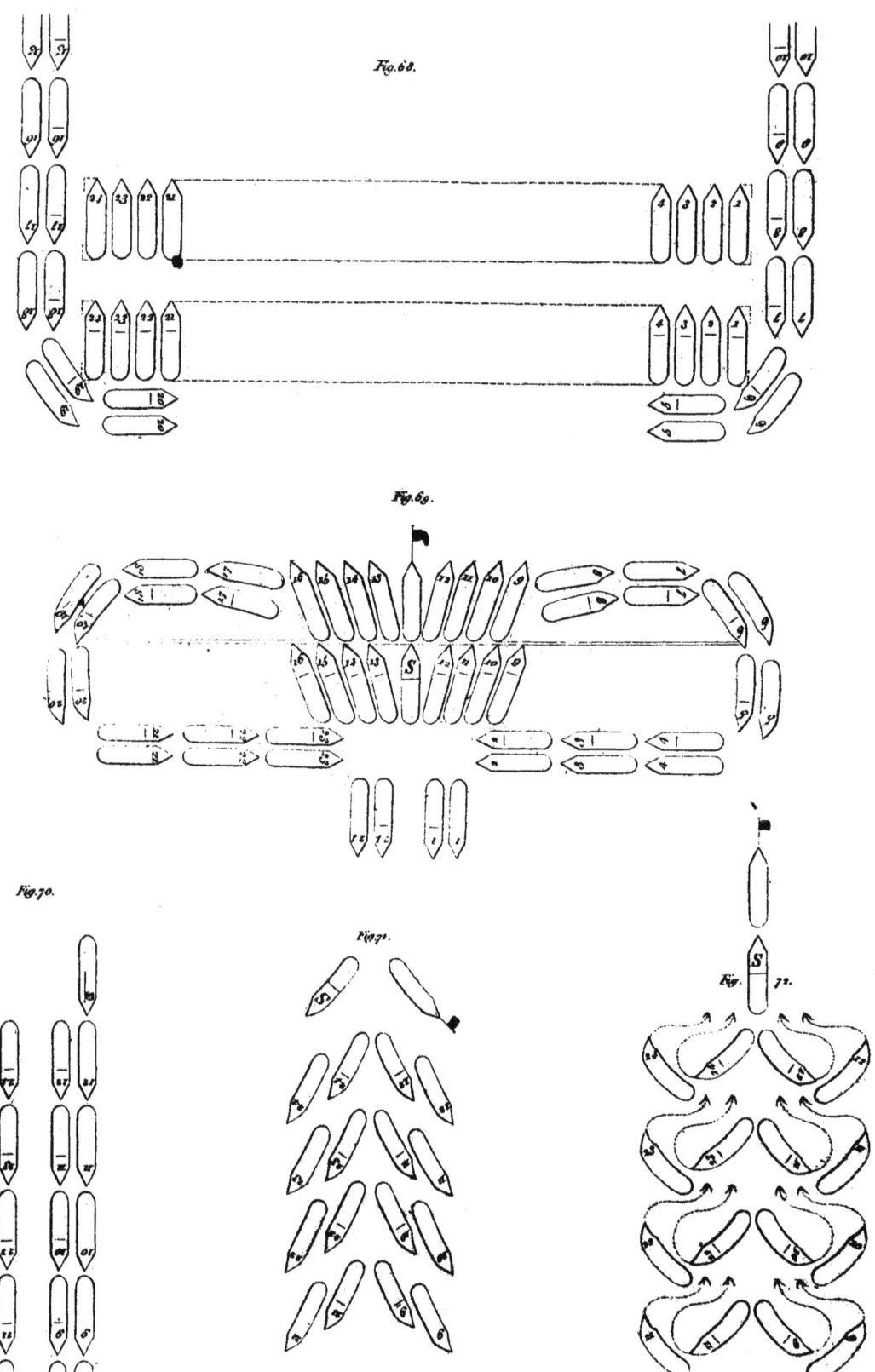

PLATE XV.

SECT. LXVIII. *From both Flanks File to the Rear.*

This is explained before. The flank officers, who lead the files from the flanks, have the charge of leading straight that they may never diverge, or converge, in which case they could not form regularly.

The leading the flanks in parallel lines is most essential: and can only be done by the following method:—

That flank to which they were dress'd before filing, is to be the directing flank; and the leader must take two or more objects in his sight in a direct line, and keep them in that line in his march. The leader of the other flank must keep his eye on the directing flank, and carefully preserve his distance.

SECT. LXIX. *Form Inwards to your former Front. (Or Bugle Signal.)*

The right half squadron forms to the right about, the left half squadron to the left about. [*Fig.* 68.]

The reader is referred to the caution and directions relating to the last two figures.

SECT. LXX. *From both Flanks form Column of Fours to the Rear.*

They file to the rear as before, but following close to the croup of the leading files, who wheel inwards round the croups of the rear rank, meeting in the centre of the rear; then wheeling from the squadron, march on in a column [*Fig.* 69.] leaving a space between the half squadrons in column equal to the width of one horse, (just as in the column of *Fig.* 65.) The standard and his covering serjeant file off with the right half squadron, and when in column they cover the two outer men, as in [*Fig.* 70.] which represents the rear of the column.

SECT. LXXI. *About outwards Singly (Or Bugle Signal to Rally).*

On the word or commencement of the signal, [*Note.*] they are to halt, and loosen their files by inclining outwards. The front rank men advancing half a horse's length at the same time inclining outwards, as in [*Fig.* 71.] When the bugle ceases they all go about outwards singly; that is, the right half squadron to the left about, the left half squadron to the right about, every man on his own ground: as in [*Fig.* 72.]

The space left in the midst of the column makes this easier, as the croups of the rear rank are less confined.

It is evident that the rear-rank men cannot go about till their front-rank men have made room for them; which they are very apt to neglect, and thus the evolution becomes difficult and irregular, and the horses are terribly justled and made unsteady. By means of the front rank men advancing as here directed, a great deal of room is gained, and time of course. The croup of the horse so advanced, clears the head of the rear rank horse sooner by half a length. In a defile the space is of importance; besides which, if the horse merely opens outwards, he must back or passage into his place again; whereas by the means here directed, all his motion is circular and advancing, which is much easier; and as soon as the rear rank horse has cleared the croup of the front rank horse, they wheel up together.

Some further observations on turning a horse round, will be found in the next plate.

It generally happens that when the flank men file off, the horses, whose turn is not yet come to move off, are impatient to turn, and drive their croups upon the others in rank. The riders must prevent this by putting on smartly the opposite leg, and even making them *passage* off the first step or two.

[*Note—Commencement of the signal.*] When signals are given by the bugle, the men are to prepare on the commencement of the signal, and to execute at the close of it. It is like the effect of the caution, and the word "March" in words of command.

PLATE XVI.

SECT. LXXIII. [*The Squadron being in Column of Fours as in Fig.* 65.]
To the Right about Form Squadron.

The leading four, front and rear, with the standard and covering serjeant, wheel altogether on the right flank man to the right about. The right half squadron forms on their right hand by coming singly into their places and facing to the right about. The left half squadron inclines, or wheels by files successively, to the left, sufficiently to leave room for the right half squadron to form, and marches all round the intended line of formation till arrived at the croups of their leading files and then forms on them. [*Fig.* 74.]

In Sect. 27 and 35, it has been mentioned, that when filed from the left flank they are seldom formed to the *right-about*. In the present instance it becomes necessary. The right half-squadron is filed from the *left* flank, and it must be formed to the *right about*. It is difficult, because the turn is so considerable, and it must be executed with much precision. If any attempt to form before it comes to their turn, all is confusion. In one material respect the instructions given for this formation must be different from those for forming to the front, viz. that (as the rear rank has to advance further than the front rank, and into the place the front rank would occupy if forming to the front) the *front-rank* man has to halt at the *head* of the horses in rank, and let his *covering file* pass him (see No. 6, front and rear rank in the Fig.) just as in other formations it has been directed, that the *rear-rank* man should halt at the *croup* of those in rank to let his file *leader* pass him.

This formation may be of use to front and defend a defile (as a bridge for example) which a column of fours is passing.

SECT. LXXIV.

In plates 14 and 15, two columns of fours have been shewn, of different kinds. The one [*Fig.* 65.] with the centre men of the squadron leading, the other [*Fig.* 69 and 70] with the flanks of the squadron leading. They are convertible one into the other, by the files going about outwards singly. But while in their original position, it is obvious that they must form in very different ways.

Thus if the column of fig. 70 (the flanks leading) should be formed instead of countermarched, if to form to the former front, the half squadrons must wheel outwards by files, each to the extent of its own front, then the right half squadron forming to the left, and the left half squadron forming to the right, the squadron will be in its original position. If they are to make front to the rear, (the right half squadron being now on the left, and the left half squadron on the right) one must halt, let the other advance a few paces sufficiently to clear them, each form separately, and when formed, change places by wheeling by threes; then wheel up and bring the rear half squadron forwards into line.

A column of fours to the rear, may be formed very properly by wheeling the squadron about by threes—advancing to the centre men (the covering serjeant and rear centre men leading) just as when formed to the front in [*Fig.* 64, and 65.] and the column may form squadron precisely in the same way as that column has done, and threes wheel up when formed.

SECT. LXXV.

Having mentioned in a preceding page (sect. 71.) that much ground and time may be lost or saved by the different modes of turning a horse round, and as the subject will in subsequent pages be found material in the instructions for wheeling, &c. we shall here take the liberty to quit the *drill* for a short time, and enter on the *manege*, as far as connected with the horse evolutions.

At first sight it would scarcely be imagined, that there were various modes of turning a horse round the same way; as, to the right about for example: yet it will immediately appear to be the case, when we place horses in different situations relative to obstacles before, or behind them, or on their right or left.

Let fig. 75 represent a quadrangle (as a riding house.) There are nine situations in which a horse may be placed in it.

Now it is plain, that No. 1. standing with his *head* to one wall and his *left side* to another, if facing to the right about, must turn in a manner very different from that of No 9. standing with his *croup* and *right side* to the walls. The same must be observed of those standing in the other angles. Those standing next to the centres of the walls are more at liberty, and the one in the centre of the riding house, is quite at liberty to turn in any way.

No. 5 then may turn on his own centre (like the figure A in the same plate) his fore legs describing one semi-circle, his hind legs another. He may turn on his fore legs, while his croup describes a semi-circle, (as at C—called in the manege the *pirouette*)

Pl. 16.

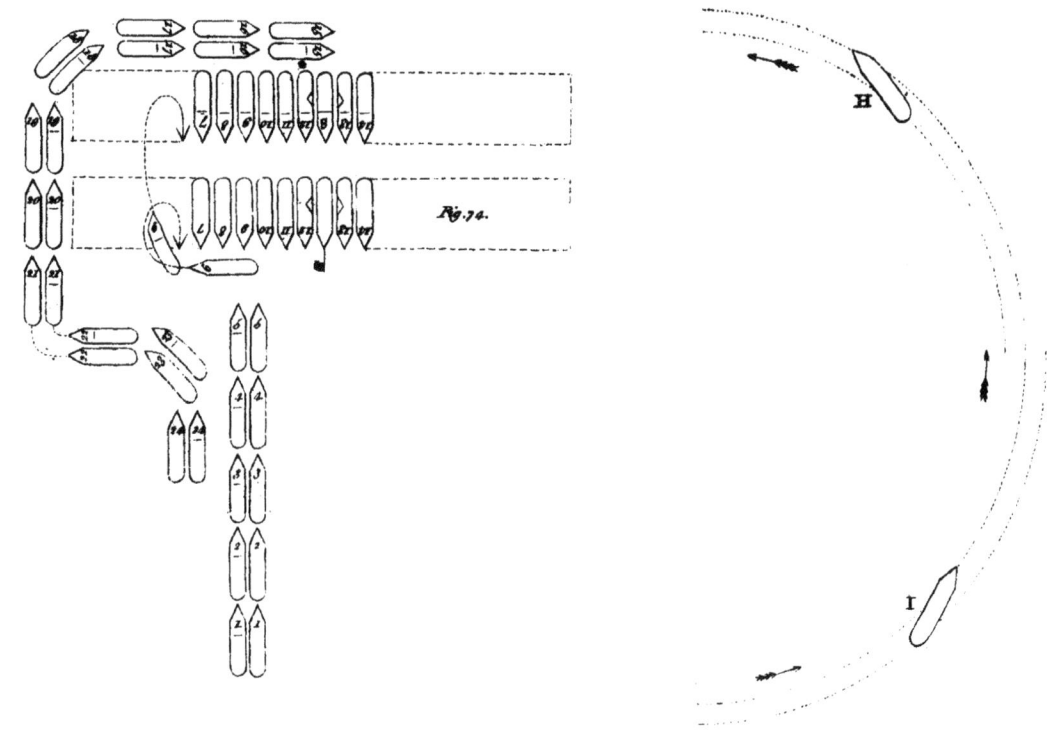

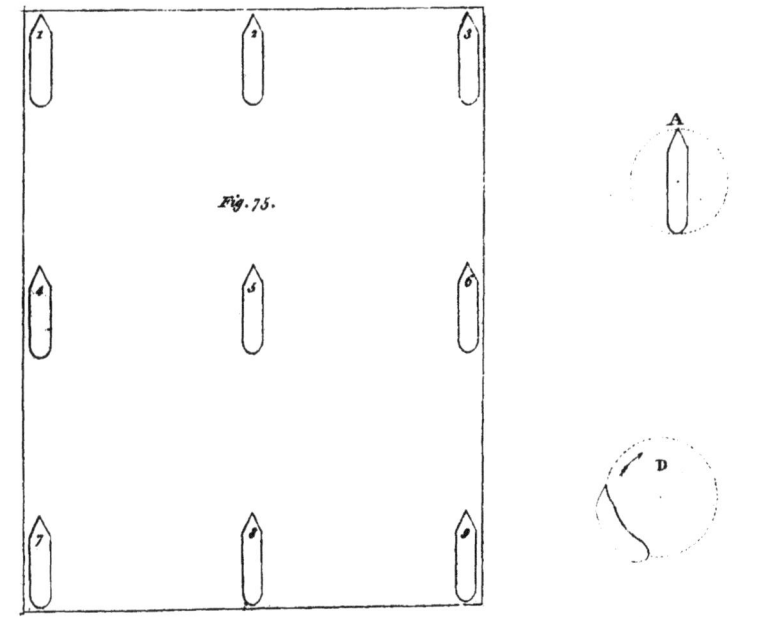

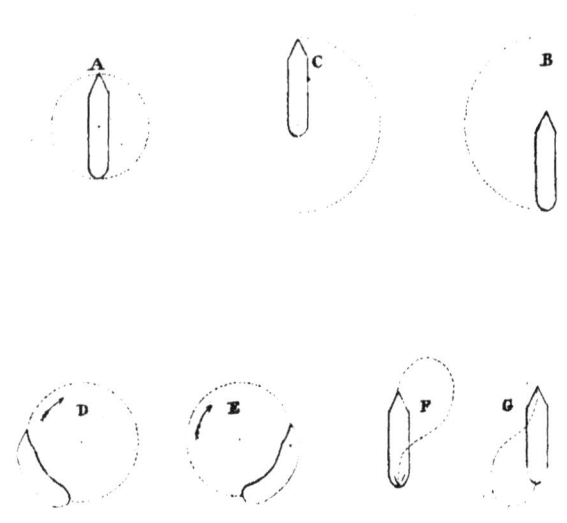

and then rein back into his place. He may incline to the left and advance in a circle, as at D, or in like manner incline to the right and rein back in a circle (E); without passing in either case, before or behind the ground he before stood on.—He may advance, and move circularly to the right (as at F), or rein back circularly towards his left (as at G)—or he may move in a direction compounded of two or more of these several actions. All this is in facing to the *right* about. The same may be done in facing to the *left* about.

The other horses may take, some one, some more of these methods of turning, but no other can take them all. Those, with their heads to the wall, of course cannot advance; nor can those, with their croups to the wall, retire. Those on the *right* side of the riding-house cannot turn to the right on their *hind* legs, nor those on the *left* side on their *fore* legs. None of the four in the angles or the two at the sides, can turn on their centres.

These turns are termed in the manege *demivoltes*; a *volte* being a turn of a *whole circle*.

Large circles are not termed *voltes*.

A volte or demivolte may be of one track, or of two tracks *(à une piste, ou à deux pistes)*. The former is where the hind-feet exactly follow the fore-feet—the latter, where the fore-feet describe one track on the ground, the hind-feet another.

Large circles also may be of one track or of two. In a circle of two tracks the fore-feet may describe the larger and the hind-feet the smaller circle, (as at H) or the fore-feet may describe the smaller and the hind-feet the larger (as at I).

A horse may also move *a deux pistes*, (in two tracks) in a right line, as in passaging; i. e. moving sideways to the right or left. [Note 1.]

A horse's head should always be turned the way he is to move, except when reining back.

It seems unnecessary to encumber the above observations with the production of authorities, because no disputable point is entered upon.

In circles, if the horse is to move in two tracks, with the croup *in*, the bridle-hand must be carried inwards, and the *outer* leg put on. There are few occasions on which this ought to be practised. (Note 2) At setting off in a gallop it may, in order to make the horse gallop (as he ought always to do) with his inner leg foremost; but the moment he has set off right, he should be made to feel the pressure of the inner leg of his rider; that he may be obliged either to make his circle of one track, (the hind-legs following exactly the fore-legs, and his body bending in a small degree to correspond with the circle described) or to move with his croup outward. It is impossible for a horse to move swiftly in a circle, without leaning inwards. This tends to throw him on his side, his feet slipping outwards and flying up. A horse never seems to guard against the slipping of his feet: he will lean as much on wet and slippery turf, as he would on the firmest ground. Now if his croup is within the circle, by leaning inwards (which he must always do,) his body is advanced in the direction in which he is moving, before his legs: whereas if his croup is out, by leaning inwards, his legs go on in that direction before his body, (i. e. farther advanced towards that part of the circumference of the circle to which his motion is directed). In the former case the centre of gravity is beyond the support, in the latter behind it; and no argument is necessary to prove which is the firmest position. Add to this, that as every degree of velocity throws the body moving, *from* the centre of the circle, if his haunches are *out*, his weight is thrown on them, as it ought always to be.

When a horse is to make a circle of two tracks with his croup *outwards* (which, as we have said, ought always to be the case, except for the purpose of a lesson to the horse) the *inner* leg must be put on—the bridle-hand carried *outwards* in a horizontal position, with the lower side (i. e. the little finger) outwards, the *back* of the hand, if the circle is to the *left*, carried *undermost*, if to the *right*, *uppermost*. This position of the hand, by shortening the inner rein, will bend the horse's neck *in*. Yet the hand, being carried all together over the outward shoulder, presses the inner side of the jaw more than the outer side; and thus serves as a signal for him to carry out his croup. Instructions on this subject are given in Lord Pembroke's Military Equitation, and in Berenger's Art of Horsemanship.

[Note 1.] The word "passage" in the old manege has a different signification: but is now commonly used in the sense here annexed to it.

[Note 2.] (A circle *à deux pistes croup en dedans.*) The occasional practice of it, however, in the riding-house, if well managed, has one excellent effect, viz. that of throwing the horse's legs out before him. Lord Pembroke says, it is particularly advantageous for horses that are apt to throw themselves forwards.

Lord Pembroke says a horse ought never to be turned without first moving a step forwards. Every observation of this nobleman on the subject, is worthy of attention. When there is room for the horse to advance, the action will be more easy, speedy, and graceful. This is the motion directed above in Sect 70. (Note 3.)

Col. Tyndale says (Mil. Equit. page 53) that a "horse should never turn on his fore legs, if it can possibly be avoided, but there should be described a circle round the hind-legs." This is the pirouette above mentioned.

We do not however see in what part of military evolutions the pirouette can be used---it is a very difficult air; and a horse will not put it in practice, if (as directed in another page in the same work) the leg, when put on, is " *carried well back*," which certainly presses away the *croup*, not the *shoulders*. If a horse's head (the horse being supposed suppled and taught) is turned to the left with the bridle, the left leg put on pressing away his croup, he turns to the left on his fore-feet. If the hand is a little eased and the other leg presses a *little* at the same time (but not so much as the left leg) he moves forward circling to the left ---in one or two tracks, according to the proportionate pressure of the legs, and slackness or tightness of the bridle. If, while the head is still carried to the left, the *right* leg is put on, (the croup by these means pressed the same way with the head) the horse passages.

The last mentioned author in the same passage observes that " turning on the fore-legs is in some cases unavoidable, as in the centre horse of threes, when endeavouring to turn on his own ground." In the Cavalry Regulations too, it is directed, that the centre horse of threes should wheel on his fore-legs. Capt. Neville in a treatise on the Discipline of Light Cavalry, (an intelligent work, which, though not in every part coinciding with the Cavalry Regulations since published, contains many instructions that may be particularly useful to officers of volunteer corps) directs that the *left* of threes, (when wheeling to the right) should turn on his fore-legs, *the centre* and right *reining back*. However, we cannot but differ, on this point, from all the above authorities; conceiving it demonstrable that the *centre* horse of threes ought to wheel on a central point, between the extremities of his nose and his croup: and for our argument refer our reader to fig. 4, in plate 1, to the notes to sect. 5 and 6, and to plate 12, and explanation. It is not to be understood, that it is here expected the horses should move with the exactness of machines, but let us be exact in theory, and come as near as we can in practice. If the *attempt* is incorrect, the execution must deviate still more.

Let a horse be placed in a riding-house, in the position of No. 4. fig. 75---mark the wall, just before his nose, and behind his tail---measure the centre between the marks---that centre will be just behind the girths: face him about, and place his nose and croup to the same marks---the centre spot will still come behind the girths. But if a horse is faced about on his fore-feet, he will stand three feet backwarder than before, as may be proved by making marks in the like manner. This is exactly as mentioned by Capt. Neville, for he says the centre and right of threes must rein back to keep parallel with the left of threes, facing to the right on his fore-legs. As he distinguishes in the same passage between a column of march and of manœuvre, it seems his reason for this direction is, that the alignement should be preserved by the *body* of the rider, who then becomes the pivot man; whereas, in the wheeling here directed, the side of the horse comes where the heads of the horses were: and of course the bodies of the riders (pivots) are advanced beyond their original alignement. This however will be the case in a *greater degree* under the directions of the Cavalry Regulations: and, according to Capt. Neville's mode, as the squadron will stand three feet more to the rear of the column, how shall it be practised if the right *half* squadron only wheel by threes to the right? still less can it be done if the half squadrons wheel by threes *outwards*.

Though unwilling to be prolix, we must take this opportunity of again mentioning the subject of the seat. Many gentlemen (who really take pains) are apt to squeeze their thighs together so as to raise the breech in some degree from the saddle. This position is not easy to themselves---it is very stiff in appearance---and not the true seat. They should *open* the thighs, hollowing the back till the breech falls close into its place in the saddle, then turning them a little inwards, gently close them without force, the legs hanging easily from the knees and moveable, The body not perpendicular, but inclining backwards. The whole weight of the body should be entirely on the saddle. The stirrups should support merely the weight of the legs. The knees and thighs should support nothing. This is not advanced as a new or disputed opinion; it is directed by all the authors above quoted, and by all intelligent riding masters. Stiffness is not firmness, but the contrary. A firm seat consists in a ready balance; and a ready and habitual balance, on an uncertainly moving support, can only be acquired by pliability of body and practice. A sailor keeps his legs on deck in the most violent tossing of the ship without any reflection on the subject; how, but by yielding to the motion? A statue would be overthrown by the slightest roll. It is said (and truly) that the thighs should be immoveable while the legs and body are moveable; but it is not possible that a man should never be put out of his position, yet, by aiming at it always, he finds it again readily, and it becomes habitual.

Note 3.] An observation made above in a note to the preface, viz. that " a horse ought not to be much on his haunches in reining back" is advanced, with submission, because it appears to differ from this noble author and also from Berenger's Art of Horsemanship. A well taught, active, and supple horse, performing his airs in the manege, may poise himself in the manner mentioned by Lord Pembroke and Berenger; and even trot backwards with much grandeur and elegance---but, for common purposes, we cannot but think (notwithstanding the deference justly due to these authorities) that the less a horse sinks on his haunches in reining back, the better: for the reasons given in the note above-mentioned. In another instance we may seem to differ from Lord Pembroke; but it is only in degree, not in substance; and that variation arising probably from the difference of situations of the persons to whom this work is addressed. His lordship directs, that in all the turnings, passaging, &c. the horse should be guided (*when possible*) by the hand only, and not the leg: the frequent use of which he condemns very much. This is certainly just, if intended of a horse with a nice mouth, and a rider with the nice hand, that might be expected from Lord Pembroke's manege; but with respect to the horses of volunteer corps, (and perhaps of the regulars,) if we can get them all to *obey* the leg, " *est quoddam prodire tenus*": to do *without* it, is more than can be expected.

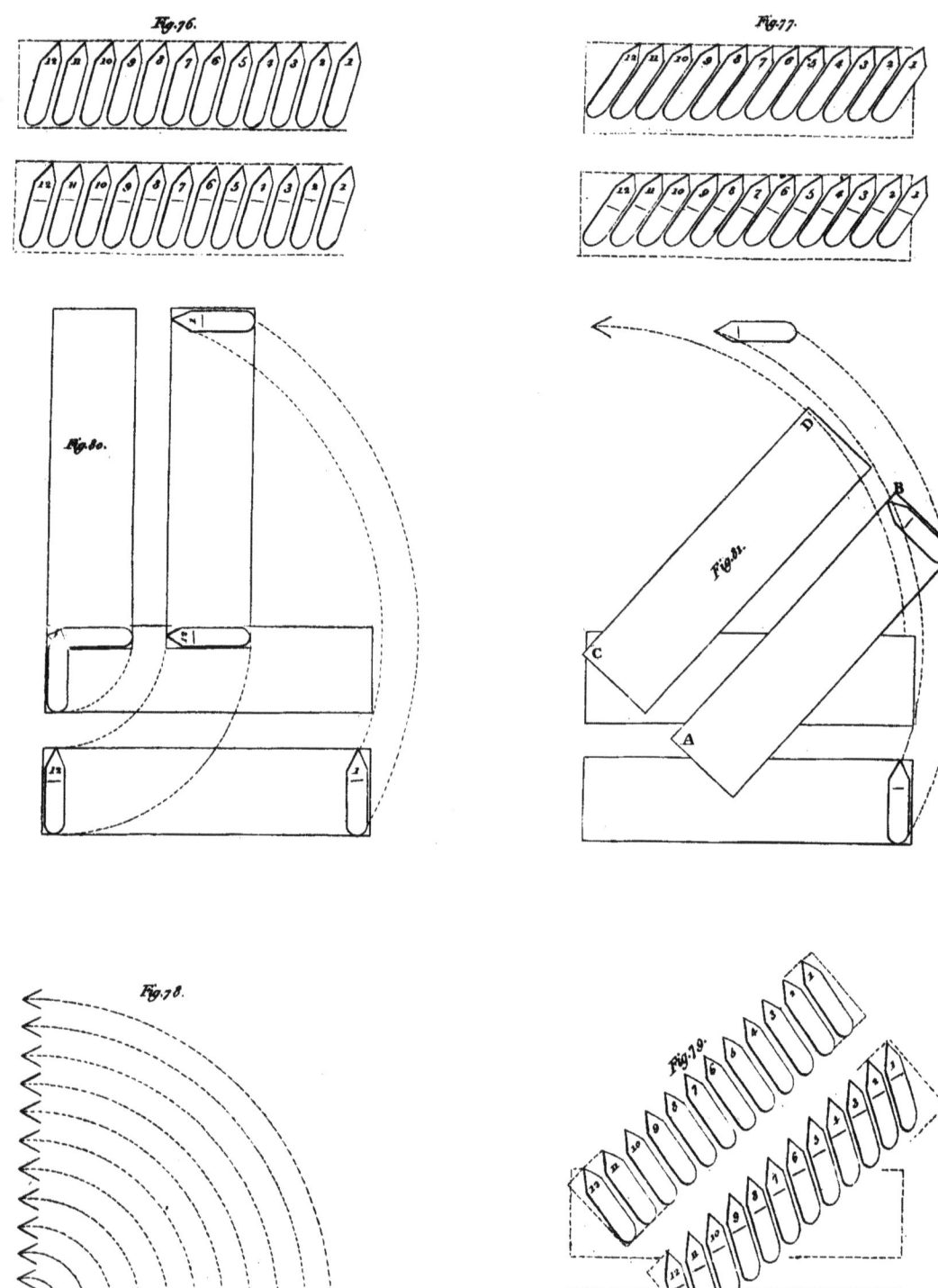

PLATE XVII.

(The Squadron supposed marching to the Front.)

SECT. LXXVI.—*Right incline.*

Eyes right immediately (without waiting for orders.)

The whole carrying their bridle hands to the right, and gently putting on the right leg, incline their horses all carefully in the same degree.

Their front remaining parallel to the former front [as in *Fig.* 76 and 77.]

> The degree of inclination will depend on the officer who leads. It is observable that the greater the degree of inclination the closer the files will be (the front not extending.) In [*Fig.* 76] a line drawn lengthwise through one horse, forms an angle of 17 degrees with the perpendicular (or line at right angles with the front). In *Fig.* 77, 34 degrees. The latter will bring the files so close that they cannot incline more without extending the front.

> In the Cavalry Regulations it is said, that " on the order to *incline*, each man makes a half face on his horse's fore-feet." The word *half*-face cannot be understood literally: for in the same section it is observed that " the distance of files at six inches allows the squadron to incline in perfect order, *while its new direction does not pass an angle of* 34° with respect to its former one," whereas a *half*-face would form an angle of 45°. The same observation will apply to the direction in the Cavalry Regulations for wheeling by twos; where it is said " the flank man of each two will *half* turn on his horse's forefeet, and the other man will *half* wheel up: which it is impossible for them to do for want of room.

> According to the degree of inclination, the rear-rank will cover more or less to the right of their file-leaders. In *Fig.* 76 they cover the man on the right of the leading-file. In [*Fig.* 77.] they cover the third man from their file-leader. Any of the intermediate degrees will bring them to cover either intermediate intervals or files. This is a very useful movement, and requires great nicety. Men are apt to dress by some rule they have adopted respecting the relative situation of their horses' heads – which come of course upon the neck or shoulders of the right-hand horse; or by their boot-tops—which, in some degrees of inclining, fall under the knee of the right-hand man: but all these are false helps, and lead them into curves and irregular lines, at a time when a true line is of the utmost importance. The same mode of dressing must be observed as in other positions; and men must (as on all occasions) be careful to correct their errors *immediately*, but *slowly*. An almost *imperceptible* quickening or slackening of pace brings them into line; a small degree more carries the correction beyond what was intended, and deceives others at the same time: for men must recollect, that as they fluctuate, others dressing by them fluctuate in an increased proportion.

> Any degree of inclination may be used, till the heads and necks of the horses lie almost against the haunches of the horses on their right; but in this case the front becomes very much extended, and it can only be done by increasing the degrees of inclination in succession from the flank inclined to.

At the word

Front, (or, if marching, Forward,)

They put on the left legs, carry the bridle-hand to the left, and are square to the front: eyes turned immediately to the point to which they were directed before inclining.

> The great use of this movement is thus explained in the Cavalry Regulations:—" It is of great use in the marching of the line in front to correct irregularities that may happen," (e. g. in column, to correct the alignement of pivots; in line, to enlarge or diminish the interval between squadrons, &c.) " It is equivalent to the oblique marching of infantry. It enables to gain the enemy's flank without exposing your own, and without wheeling, or altering the parallel front of the squadron." It is also frequently used to diminish or increase the front of a column; as will be shewn in another page.

Wheeling.

SECT. LXXVII.—*Left Wheel.*

On the caution to wheel to the *left*, all turn eyes to the *right*: the right (or wheeling) flank-man only excepted, who dresses inwards by the left (or pivot) flank-man.

March.

The man on the left (or pivot) flank, turns his horse on his fore-legs to the left. The wheeling flank man moves forwards at a brisk pace, circling to the left. All the rest with eyes to the right, left legs put on, bridle hands carried as before described, to oblige the horse to carry his croup out from the centre, advance in concentric circles parallel to the right-flank man, [see *Fig.* 78.] and when they have wheeled the quarter circle, receive the word

Halt—Dreſs,

Which instantly obeying, they dress immediately by the man on the standing flank who has never quitted his ground.

The word "HALT" must be given *before* the wheel is completed; that none may overshoot and have occasion to rein back. Then they dress up immediately.

[*Fig.* 78] represents the wheel of a single rank. [*Fig.* 80] by lines only on which the two ranks are supposed to be formed, serves to shew the relative position of the front and rear rank before and after the wheel. The pivot flank horse turning on his fore legs, describes a quarter circle with the croup: this is the motion of B [Plate 16]. The next to him by keeping parallel must make a quarter volte of two tracks—croup out. The rest in like manner, progressively, in larger voltes or circles.

The wheel of the rear-rank is more difficult: for they wheel on a point not within their own rank, but advanced considerably in their front, viz. the fore-legs of the front-rank pivot horse. In [*Fig.* 80] the dotted curves between No. 12 and No. 12, shew the direction of the head and croup of the horse covering the pivot. It is also a circle of two tracks, with the croup so much out as to point directly from the centre of the circle—which is, in fact, *paſsaging* circularly. This motion is slow, his circle being small. The same figure by dotted curves between No. 1 and No. 1, shews the direction of the head and croup of the rear-rank horse covering the wheeling flanker: which is a larger circle not concentric with that of No. 12. for the centre of the circle is in the front-rank, (as at C. *Fig.* 81.) This is also a circle of two tracks, croup outwards. Inasmuch as in this circle the croup is not so much outward as in the former, it is easier: but as it must be made much more rapidly, it is more difficult. In all the intermediate places the speed and the degree of passaging are proportionate; the former diminishing, the latter increasing, as we reckon inwards. [*Fig.* 81) is like the former, but representing a *half* wheel. (Note.] C is the point on which the whole turns as on a centre. The line A B must be kept parallel to the line C D in every part of the wheel while in motion; as well as on the halt.

[Note, *half-wheel*.] A half, quarter, eighth, or sixteenth wheel, signifies that portion of the quarter circle. Wheeling *about* describes a semicircle.

These positions are what men must *attempt* and bring about as nearly as they can. But horses cannot be made to gallop or advance *fast* with the croups out of the circle in any great degree, and therefore they must incline. The less they incline the better; but as much as they do, so much must they cover beyond their leading-file, [as in *Fig.* 79.] Thus at the instant of the halt, they will be ready to *front* (as before shewn under the head of inclining) and will cover their proper file-leaders: this must be understood of directions given " to cover away well to the wheeling flank," not that they are to keep the *croups back* but the *heads forward*—for the croups ought at least to be kept up to the perpendicular position, and if beyond it, the movement is better executed.

In the Cavalry Regulations it is directed, that the croups should be lightly closed *inwards*. We must take the liberty to dissent from this for the reasons above given.

It is also said in the same section that the rear-rank must *rein back* at the standing flank, which is not easily understood; for they are certainly advancing, though not in a direct line. Probably it means they should *passage*, as above shewn.

Capt. Neville gives the same directions as in these pages.

There is a deception in the appearance of this movement in the rear-rank; for men forgetting that the centre of their circle is in the front-rank, begin turning as if on a point within their own; then finding themselves left behind out of the line of their file-leaders, are obliged to incline suddenly and irregularly to regain their position: and even if done rightly, the eye is deceived, for they appear to be circling with the croup in, when they are not. Thus in [*Fig.* 79] all the rear-rank appear to have the croups *in*; whereas, if one point of a pair of compasses be fixed on that spot on which the fore-feet of the pivot horse may be supposed to stand, the other point of the compasses will shew, that No. 1. the wheeler (rear-rank) has his croup *on* the same circumference with his head, and that No. 12. has it in a very great degree *outward*: the rest in the intermediate proportions. If the horse No. 1. is sufficiently supple to carry his croup more out (like B in *Fig.* 81) he ought to do it, and the rest to conform.

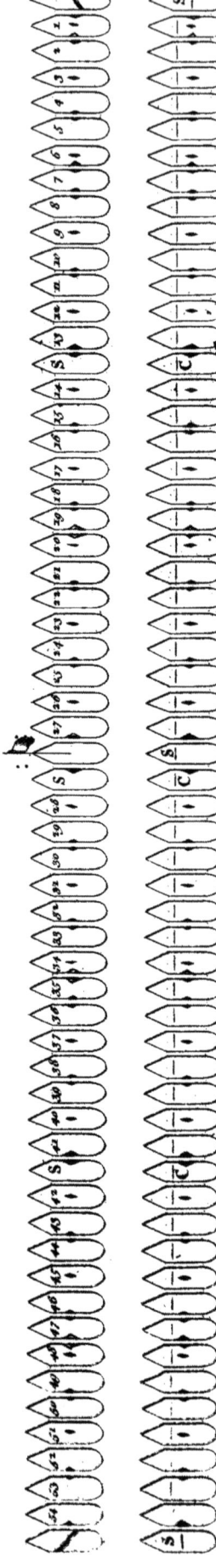

Fig. 83.

Fig. 82.

PLATE XVIII.
SECT. LXXVIII.

[*Fig.* 82.] Represents a squadron formed, officers and non-commissioned officers posted, and the squadron told off in half squadrons, divisions, subdivisions and ranks by threes.

Two troops compose a squadron. Two or more squadrons a regiment. Two or more regiments a line. [Cavalry Regulations]

The troops are formed first separately. On the signal (trumpet or bugle) the second officer of the troop takes his stand on the right of the intended line of formation, and the men form on him in rank entire as directed Sect. 1. [*Fig.* 1.] The senior officer of the troop (then in front of the line), by changing the situation of men according to the height of man and horse together, sizes from flank to flank: that troop which is to compose the right half squadron, has the tallest on the left, the other on the right; so that the tallest men will be in the centre of the squadron, decreasing gradually to the flanks. [Note 1.] Then the rear rank is formed at close order as directed in (Sect. 2 and 3 *Fig.* 2.) [Note 2.] The troops are then closed together, in any way most convenient, as by passaging, filing, or wheeling by threes, and wheeling up: when the senior officer of the two troops, (except in a regiment when a field officer commands a squadron) takes his post one horse's length in front of the centre. The men then number themselves from right to left, as in Sect 5. and from the number of the last man, the officer knows the strength of his squadron. He places the officer carrying the standard in the centre of the front-rank, covered by a non-commissioned officer. He has then three non-commissioned officers to place in the front rank, and adding them in his mind to the number of the left flank man, he divides the sum into halves, (half squadrons), quarters, (divisions), and eighths, (subdivisions). But as his centre-division must divide into threes, if the true quarter of the squadron will not so divide, he adds one, or two, and posts a serjeant (included in the reckoning) on the right of each centre division. Then he places a third serjeant on the right of the left division. These serjeants are covered by corporals. [Note 3.] By these means, if the original quarter of the number of the squadron was a sum not divisible by threes, the flank divisions will be weaker than the centre divisions. This will always be the case, when the whole number is not divisible by 12; as 48, 60, 72. If the squadron exceeds in number 47 files, he halves the divisions. If the divisions consist of an odd number, the subdivisions nearest to the centre should be the strongest. If the squadron is of less than 48 files, he must not sub-divide: for less than six files cannot act as a subdivision; as will presently be shewn.

The senior officer of each troop (or if one of them is the squadron officer, then the next senior officer) takes his post on the outer flank of his own troop, and is covered by a non-commissioned officer.

In the Plate [*Fig.* 82] the flank-officers are distinguished by a waving band—the squadron officer by two bands crossed—the standard-officer by a small flag. Serjeants and corporals, by the letter S. and C. [Note 4.] The rear ranks and the threes as in former plates. The right of divisions and subdivisions by an additional half diamond on the right, the left of divisions and subdivisions by the like on the left; and to assist the eye in finding them, two small dots are placed in the front and rear between the divisions, and one between the subdivisions.

[Note 1.] The sizing the squadrons, is not a matter of mere parade, but greatly assists the dressing. In the regulars they are sized in the roll, and therefore the time saved on duty: but the uncertain attendance of Volunteer Corps and their frequent and optional change of horses, renders the operation necessary at every meeting. It will also be necessary to put slow or unsteady horses in the rear.

[Note 2.] Capt. Neville (in his work before quoted) directs the rear rank to be formed by reining back half the front rank after sizing; then passaging, or filing them into their places: but the effect of this will be, that the centre men of the rear rank in squadron will be shorter than the flank men of the front rank; whereas the covering file ought to be one that can properly take the place of his front rank man if occasion requires.

[Note 3.] It is thus directed in the Cavalry Regulations. But as there are 16 non-commissioned officers to each squadron, (viz. 8 in each troop) it may be well in Volunteer Corps to place additional ones (included in the telling off) on the left flanks of divisions.

[Note 4.] There is no occasion in Volunteer Corps for distinction between serjeant and corporal; but by making use of the letters S. and C. in the plates, the rear rank non-commissioned officers *told in* are distinguished from those covering the standard and flank officers, and which are not told in. And these latter are distinguishable from the front rank serjeants by having the rear rank mark on them. In the Cavalry Regulations, the officers are covered by corporals—in the Elucidation of the Cavalry Regulations by serjeants; the latter is usually practised.

In the plate of the Cavalry Regulations Elucidated, there must be an error; as the right centre-division consists of sixteen files.

In telling off threes, twos, or fours, it has been already mentioned, that the officer must begin at the centre and tell off each half squadron separately. In the right half squadron, beginning from the standard (exclusive) he tells off thus, viz. " left, centre, right," and on the other side of the standard, " right, centre, left." Then of twos, in like manner, " right, left," and " left, right." If they are told off in threes, they should not be told off in fours.

The standard and flank officers with their covering files, are not included in the telling off by threes, twos, fours, divisions, or subdivisions.

It follows, that although it may sometimes, for the sake of saving time, be said that even numbers are left files (as in Sect. 49). yet it is not so as a matter of course. Indeed, in the regulars, the numbers are of no further consideration, than to enable the officers to tell off the divisions and to post the non-commissioned officers, and the latter are not numbered in.

Telling off by fours, instead of threes, has its advantages and disadvantages. The wheeling is not quite so ready, and it gains more on the alignement: but it leaves a greater space between head and croup when wheeled to a flank, which is better for rapid flank marches. On service, when one falls, the remaining three are capable of performing the evolutions without fresh telling off.

In the Plate, a number is purposely chosen that will make the divisions and subdivisions unequal; because it must generally happen, and it will be found that the unequal strength of divisions occasions some difference in the manœuvres, which an equal division would not have pointed out.

The number of our squadron in the plate is 54, to which add three serjeants, we have 57 files. In halves, 29, and 28. The half of 28 is 14, add one to make it divisible by three, and the centre divisions consist of 15: one flank division will have 13, the other 14. The two centre subdivisions 8, all the rest 7, except one flank subdivision which has only 6. On one flank we have two men, acting as a three, on the other a single man, acting as a three by himself: which is much better than (as sometimes practised) including him with the three next to him as a four.

Wheeling of the Squadron and its Divisions.

SECT. LXXIX. *Squadron!—Right wheel.*

On the caution the front-rank men dress by the centre; the rear rank by the left (or wheeling) flank.

March.

The squadron-officer after giving the word rides out in a circular direction preserving his distance accurately from the right (i. e. the standing) flank. The standard officer follows him and all wheel to the right preserving the same uniform front, and in the manner above directed in the section on wheeling.

The standard officer is answerable for the correctness of the circle, and for the pace, which he must so regulate as not to oblige the flank man to exceed a moderate gallop. [Cav. Reg. page 20.]

They receive the word

Halt.

Before the wheel is quite complete, and then the word

Dress,

On which the standard moves up to complete the quarter-circle, and both ranks dress by the centre.

SECT. LXXX.—*Squadron!—By Divisions—Right Wheel.*

On the caution, the serjeant covering the right flank officer marks the square of the wheel: and at the word "*march*," the four divisions wheel to the right on the officer, and the three front rank non-commissioned officers on their right flanks as pivots; who, after dressing the men by the right (or standing) flank, shift by the rear to the left flank, the serjeant on the right of the left flank division only excepted, who remains in his place, because there is an officer ready on the left flank. When the officers and serjeants have so shifted, their coverers take their places in the front rank. [*Fig.* 83.]

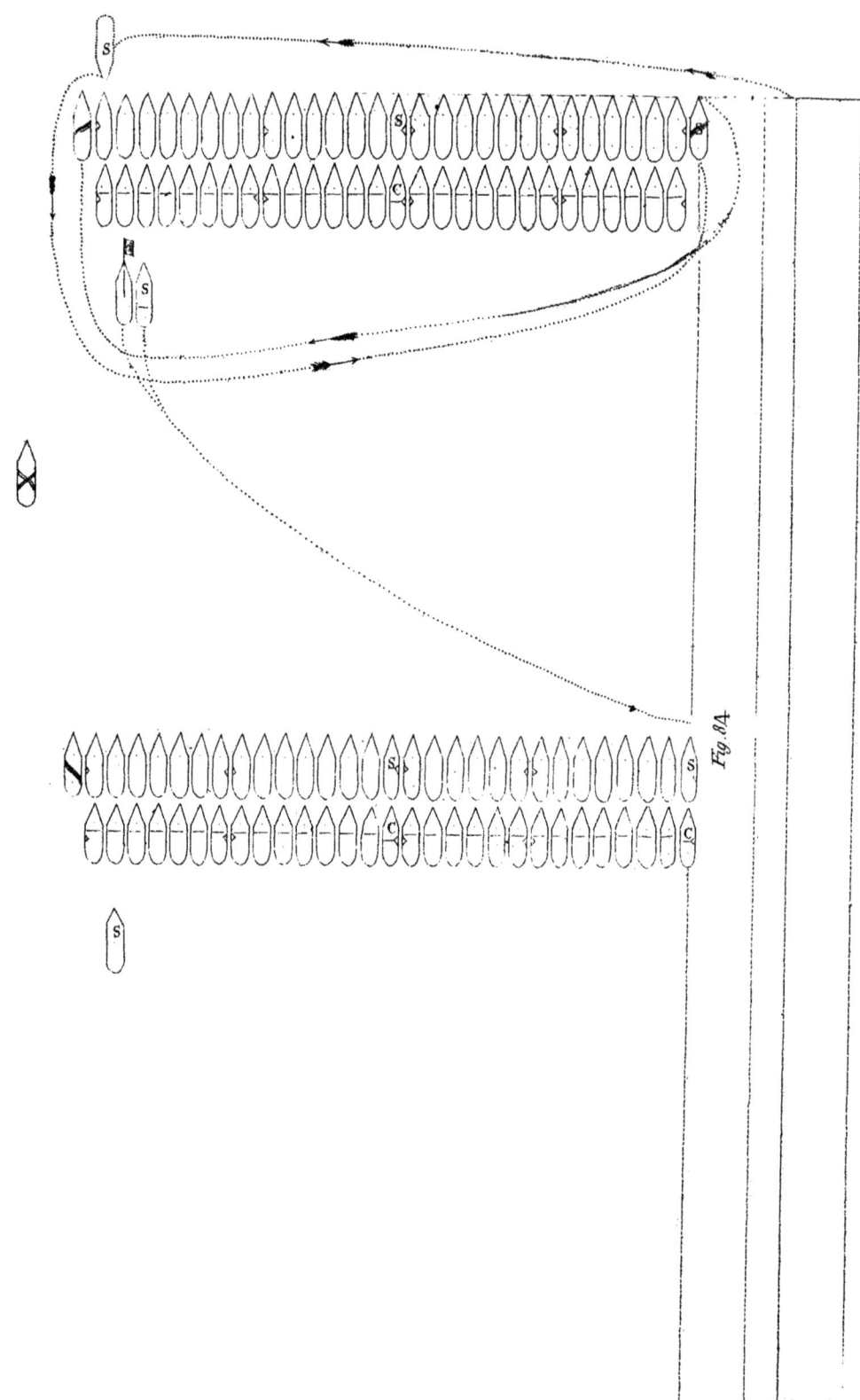

Pl. 19.

Fig. 84.

Eyes left—the left is now become the pivot-flank.

The term *pivot-flank* has been used in preceding sections, and a reference made to this part for a further explanation.

The pivot-flank, strictly speaking, is that which remains fixed, while the other wheels on it, preserving its distance accurately, and describing part of a circle, of which the pivot is the centre: the other is called the wheeling flank. But it is evident, that when the squadron has broken into any divisions, whether of half squadrons, divisions, or sub-divisions, (for all of them are called divisions of the squadron), these divisions, in order to wheel into line, must wheel on that flank as a pivot, which before was the *wheeling* flank. This flank therefore is now denominated the *pivot* flank.

It is always in the proper front.—When the right flank is leading (as when they have wheeled to the right), it is always on the left; when the left flank leads, it is always on the right. The alignement is preserved by this flank, as are the intervals between the divisions in column.

By analogy to this, in a column of sixes, or in that column of four which is formed by wheeling by twos to a flank, or in a column of eight (wheeled by fours), that flank which is to the proper front, (viz. on the left when the right flank leads, and on the right when the left flank leads) is frequently called the pivot-flank; though it is not strictly a *pivot* to be wheeled on, but by it the alignement is preserved; and to it eyes are always to be turned. It is properly termed the *directing*-flank; but the words *directing*-flank and *pivot*-flank are indiscriminately used. The other is called the *reverse*-flank.

This is an open column of divisions, right in front.

The manner of the shifting of the officers is explained in the next plate. The two serjeants who shift from the standing flanks, acting as the flank-officer does in the next figure.

Where there is a non-commissioned officer on each flank of a division, there will be no occasion for shifting: but of this they must be informed at telling off: and in such case the wheeling into line will be upon the pivot-leader, and in column his corporal must cover the second file of the rear-rank.

It must be remembered, that pivot-leaders are not to attend to the men to correct their dressing, but are to give their sole attention to their own alignement and interval; leaving the rest to the care of the non-commissioned officer on the reverse flank.

When this wheel is complete, it is observable that there will be, what are called in the Cavalry Regulations, "false intervals," (i. e.) the interval between each division will be equal to the extent of the front of the preceding division; whereas, to enable them to wheel into line, they want an interval equal to the extent of their own front. The pivots also will not cover, or be in the true alignement. Neither of these must be corrected, unless ordered, till they move forwards, and then the pivot-leaders take care by inclining and slackening pace to conform to the alignement of the leading division, and to acquire the true intervals. This interval is reckoned from front-rank to front-rank, and the space for the standard must be included.

It is also to be observed, that in all division-wheelings the rear-rank must be close to the croup, for reasons which will be given: but when the column moves forwards, the close order interval between the ranks is to be taken.

PLATE XIX.

Half Squadrons! Right Wheel.

SECT. LXXXI.

On the caution, the right flank officer's covering serjeant rides out to mark the square of the wheel, placing his horse opposite to the spot to which the wheeling flank is to arrive. All eyes to the wheeling flank, and on the word

March,

The half squadrons wheel to the right, are halted, and dress by the standing flank, even though the word "dress" happen to be omitted. Then the right flank-officer shifts in the rear of his half squadron to the left, and gives the word "eyes left" that being now the pivot flank. The serjeant, who marks the wheel, at the same time returns to his own flank, (but shifting by the rear) and takes his officer's place. In the mean time the left flank officer has wheeled with his half squadron, (Note) and gives the word "eyes left." His serjeant drops behind the second file of his half squadron. The standard is behind the second file of the leading half squadron, and his serjeant on his right behind the third. [*Fig.* 84.]

The dotted lines shew the tracks of the marker and officer shifting—the points of the arrows their direction.

It must be remembered, that the marker's position determines only the square of the wheel (i. e. the angle) not the length of the line; he will mark the spot as nearly as he can, but the wheeler's eye determines it, the circle being made truly on the pivot.

[Note.] In the Elucidation of the Cavalry Regulations, it is said that the left-flank officer is to shift to the right of his half squadron to halt and dress the men from that point: but it is difficult to see how he is to get there in time, and there is a serjeant there already for that purpose. However, this direction does not seem warranted by the Cavalry Regulations, which say that he shall wheel up with his own half squadron. The same observation applies in the wheeling by divisions.

PLATE XX.

Subdivisions!—Right Wheel—March.

SECT. LXXXII.

No marker goes out—it not being requisite in so small a front. (Cav. Reg. Elucid.) The subdivisions wheel to the right. [*Fig* 85.]

- There appears in this figure a much greater space behind the rear-subdivision of the leading half squadron, than between any other subdivisions. We have already observed that the interval between the divisions after wheeling into column, depends on the extent of front of the *preceding* divisions: but, besides that, there is the space of the standard in this place.
- The Cavalry Regulations direct, that the flank officers and their coverers, and the two centre serjeants and their coverers, shall each be on the pivot flank of a subdivision: but do not inform us how they are to be got there.
- The Cavalry Regulations Elucidated, direct, that they are to post themselves on the right of their subdivisions, (which can only be done by the rear-rank non-commissioned officers shifting after the wheel) in order to halt and correct the dressing after the wheel is made; and then shift to the left flank: though the plates seem to represent the corporals shifting at once from the *right* of *their own* division, after the wheel, in the rear of their own leading subdivisions, and in front of their rear subdivisions to the pivot flank.
- The Cavalry Regulations also direct, that, when a squadron wheels into *subdivisions*, the standard and serjeant shall march behind the second and third file from the pivot of the fourth subdivision, just as above directed in half squadrons and divisions. But all these orders leave us in a dilema. For when we reflect that the depth of a subdivision of 6 files, even when close up to the croup, (as in division wheelings we have mentioned to be necessary) is more than equal to its extent of front, it is evident that a squadron of forty eight files cannot even stand in column of subdivisions without some crowding and extent of front. A subdivision of seven files, stands just easily, without any room to spare. So that it seems impossible for the pivot-leaders to shift between them, or for the standard to march in the manner directed.
- The drawings of the Cavalry Regulations Elucidated, do not describe the proportionate depth of the two ranks, but represent divisions, &c. almost as lines: whereas, any division of a squadron is a parallelogram, a *sub*-division is a square. No subdivision can exceed 8 files, unless the squadron exceeds 60. Some one or more must be as low as 7, unless the squadron exceeds 68. In a squadron of 48 none will exceed 6.
- As the column of sub-divisions so formed must be a *close* column, the standard and serjeant ought to be upon the reverse flank; for so in the section relating to close columns the Cavalry Regulations direct; but still the officers cannot shift.
- Upon the whole, the wheeling of a squadron into sub-divisions seems as unnecessary as it is difficult; for the front of the column is scarcely greater than a column of sixes (threes wheel'd to a flank,) and the latter is formed, and squadron formed from it instantaneously. When indeed a squadron is marching in a column of divisions, if the ground requires diminution of front, they may double behind into a column of sub-divisions, the non-commissioned officers find room to shift to the pivots, and the standard to the reverse flanks. Even then, it seems they should form divisions before wheeling into line.

SECT. LXXXIII.

It will be unnecessary to give any figures of wheeling to the left. Eyes are of course to the right during the wheel—to the left upon the halt—and immediately afterwards ordered to the right, which now becomes the pivot flank. The left flank serjeant marks the wheel, then his officer shifts by the rear to the right flank, and the serjeant takes his place on the left. The standard is still behind the second file from the pivot flank of the leading centre division, and his serjeant on his left. The right flank officer on the right of his own half squadron, and his serjeant behind the second file from the pivot.

- If by divisions, the front-rank serjeants (being already on the right flanks of their divisions,) have no occasion to shift. Their corporals follow the second file from the pivot[*]; for *pivot-leaders* are never to be covered: but the corporal on the right of the left centre division must take the left of the standard serjeant, his proper place being occupied by the standard.
- If by sub-divisions, it would not be difficult for the non-commissioned officers to shift, as by wheeling on the right flanks they become disengaged: but if they are to remain on the standing flank to dress the men (as before-mentioned), and then, shift, we are reduced to our former dilemma.
- In a column of sub-divisions, the left flank leading, the front-rank officers and non-commissioned officers are to lead the pivot of their own division, and the rear-rank officers lead the preceding sub-division: except, that the officer from the left takes the leading sub-division, and his serjeant and the left-division corporal, not being wanted on the pivot-flanks, take the reverse flanks of the leading sub-divisions.

[*] The "Cavalry Regulations Elucidated," say the third, but we apprehend this is an error of the press.

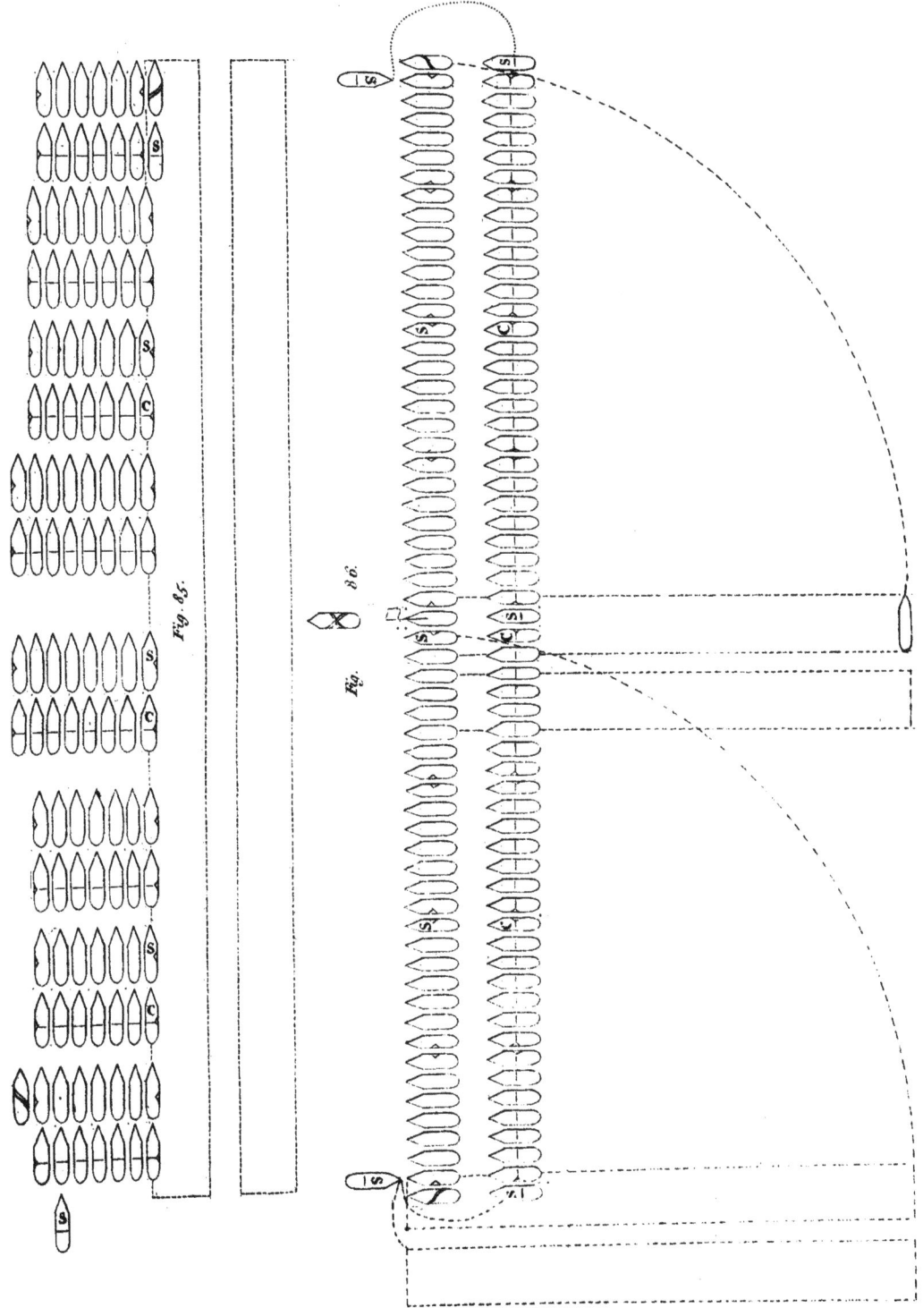

Pl 20.

Fig. 85.

Fig. 86.

Half Squadrons!—Wheel outwards.

SECT. LXXXIV.

Eyes centre.

The markers go out from both flanks, and on the word " *March,*" the right half squadron wheels to the right, the other to the left, and officers shift as before directed.

The standard and serjeant with the right half-squadron, as is always the case when the half-squadrons are separated.

It is not necessary to illustrate this by a figure.

They may wheel *about* outwards, and wheel about inwards into line: or wheel the whole circle, (i. e. about and about.)

This is of no real use as an evolution, but is calculated for practice, and performed as a proof of correctness.

Correct wheeling is very difficult. The faults most generally committed are:

1st. Flying off, or loosening out from the pivot.

2d. Crowding the pivot from his place, or forcing some out of the rank.

3d. Coming up in a semi-circle instead of a right line, by means of the centre of the rank not keeping up.

As to the first, it must be a strict rule with the pivot-man, not to quit his ground though the adjoining files quit him; but to remain firm, and oblige them to dress by him at the instant of the halt. The same rule must be observed in degree by every individual: for although they look to the wheeling flank, they must never quit the file on their pivot hand, even if they should be left by the file on their wheeling hand.

As to the second, it is principally the fault of the wheeler, who rides straight instead of circularly up to the marker—or, of the pivot-leader, who in column has not preserved his true interval for wheeling into line. In the first case, the individuals may in some measure correct it; for every one should *yield* to a pressure from the *pivot* hand, though he should not quit it; and should forcibly *resist* a pressure coming from the *wheeling* hand.

As to the third, the care must be, that all should begin the wheel instantaneously upon the word "*March;*" not waiting for the man by whom they dress, but starting with the wheeling-flank man: yet careful never to be an inch before him. The pivot flank moves very slowly—some must quite creep; which, too frequently, they are not sufficiently aware of. They must all be careful *not to lean forward* in dressing so as to see the rank, for this obstructs the sight of others: neither at starting, which habit is very common; the horse must receive his signal from the hand and legs, the body still backward in its true position.

SECT. LXXXV.—*(The Half Squadrons being wheeled to the right, as in Fig. 84.)*

Half Squadrons!—Left Wheel into Line.

The right flank-officer's serjeant marks the wheel; the left flank-officer's serjeant places his horse fronting the spot where the head of the left pivot-horse is to be. The right flank-officer shifts by the rear, from the pivot-flank to his own place; and on the word "*March,*" both half squadrons wheel to the left, and receive the word "*Halt*" each from their own leader. The standard and coverer get easily into their places during the wheel. The squadron officer rides to the left-flank to dress the men, which having done he resumes his place, and the covering serjeants theirs. [*Fig.* 86.]

SECT. LXXXVI.—*(The Divisions being wheeled to the right, as in Fig. 83.)*

Divisions!—Left Wheel into Line.

The flank-officers' serjeants place themselves as in the last section. The pivot-leaders (except the left flank-officer) shift by the rear of their divisions to the wheeling flanks, their coverers reining back into the rear-rank; and on the word "*March*" all wheel into line, and are halted by their several division-leaders—the standard and serjeant are again in the centre, and the squadron officer dresses the line as in the last section.

SECT. LXXXVII.—*(Half Squadrons or Divisions being wheeled to the left.)*

Half Squadrons! (or Divisions!)—Right Wheel into Line.

The left-flank serjeant marks the square of the wheel, and the right-flank serjeant turns out and faces the pivot.

PLATE XXI.

SECT. LXXXVIII.—*The Column! March.*

The several pivot-leaders give the word "*March,*" each to his own division: and they march forwards.

It has been observed that if the divisions of a squadron are unequal, in breaking into column of divisions, the intervals will be false, and the pivots will not cover. The pivot-leaders must therefore immediately upon the march incline till they cover exactly, and must gain an interval equal to the extent of their own division, so as to be ready to wheel up into line.

Should any intervals happen to be lost when the column halts, the pivot-leader must not correct it till the column marches again, or till ordered to dress; for that would occasion a shake in the whole column; and by correcting his defect he occasions another in his rear.

The dotted lines shew the track and covering of the pivots. [*Fig.* 87.]

Fig. 88—represents a column of sub-divisions, the pivots covering, and officers and non-commissioned officers posted as directed in the Cavalry Regulations.

The word Counter-marching may signify marching to the rear: but more technically denotes, inverting the column, line, regiment, squadron, or division, so as to change its front and flanks. Thus a column of divisions is not, properly speaking, counter-marched by any rear march of its divisions separately, nor a column of sixes (threes wheeled to a flank) by wheeling threes about; for in both, the pivot or directing flank remains to the original front; which, when the divisions wheel into line, or threes wheel up, is resumed: but it is otherwise when the leading division or the leading six wheel about, and the others follow: then when the divisions wheel into line, or threes wheel up, the front is to the former rear. So of a column of fours (form'd by wheeling by twos to a flank) as in Plate 13.

If this last-mentioned column is to retreat without counter-marching, they may wheel about by twos; and it is much better to wheel about by tows *outward*, that is (in the figure in question) the front-rank twos to the left-about, and the rear-rank twos to the right-about: and *vice versa* when the left flank leads. When a squadron is in file, upon the word "*right about counter-march*" the files wheel about, and march along by the rear as in *Fig.* 50, Plate 11: but if they are to retreat without counter-marching, they must go "*about outwards singly,*" for by wheeling like twos, their relative situations in rank would be lost.

Counter-marching and changing Front.

SECT. LXXXIX.—*(The Squadron supposed marching in a Column of Divisions right in front, as in Fig.* 87.)

Divisions will Counter-march. [*Cav. Reg. Sect.* 45.]

The non-commissioned officers from the reverse flank, shift by the rear of their respective divisions, and occupy the place of the pivot-leaders, but with their horses faced about to the intended front. The pivot-leaders at the same time shift by the front to the reverse flank, where they give the word "*right file,*" and leading from the right-flank till they observe the whole division in file, they give the word "*right about counter-march,*" lead the files round to the spot where the marker stands, and give the word "*left form,*" when they form on the left of the marker, and dress by him. Then the marker quits the position which belongs to the pivot-leader, and resumes his own.

Fig. 89, which represents the left division only, though the whole column is supposed to perform it at the same instant.

This is the mode directed in the Cavalry Regulations.

It is observable that it requires a considerable space of ground—that an inclination of the files is necessary before they can form—that the formation of the rear-rank is somewhat difficult—and that they have lost ground to the rear equal to the depth of a rank. (The space A in the figure shews the ground they have quitted.) In the Cavalry Regulations Elucidated, the extension of the division by filing to the flank is not shewn—and the figures appear to have gained ground to the front: but the contrary is evidently the case, as the front-rank stands where it was and the rear-rank has changed its place. One of these objections would be removed, by placing the marker next to the *rear*-rank man: the other can only be avoided, by adopting the mode described in the next figure.

Fig. 90, represents a division counter-marching in a manner mentioned by Capt. Neville, in his work above quoted, and which is free from these disadvantages. The marker places his horse on the flank of the rear-rank—the division first closing to the croup. Then the division advances two horses' length, and the pivot-leader files and conducts the men, as in the last section; only, as their ground is clear for them, it is not necessary to extend at all to the flank: their formation is wholly advancing, which is much easier, and they stand exactly on their original ground.

By this counter-march of the divisions, the alignement is preserved, but the intervals are false, and must be rectified in the march.—The column returns along the same ground which it had passed, and may wheel up to the same front.

Pl. 21.

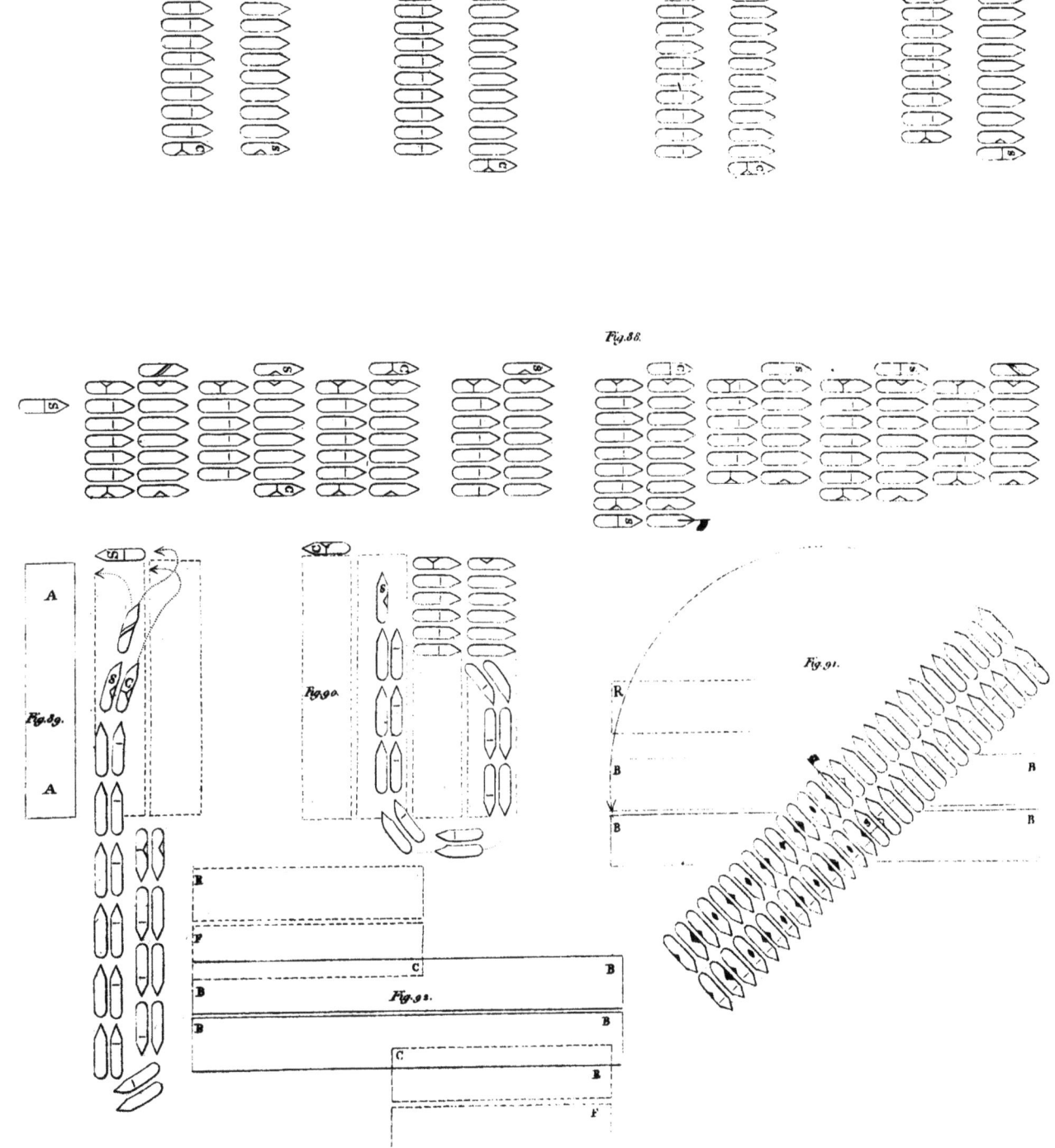

Fig. 87
Fig. 88
Fig. 89
Fig. 90
Fig. 91
Fig. 92

SECT. XC.

The Squadron changes Front by wheeling on its Centre. (Cav. Reg. Page 133.)

Left Half Squadron! By Threes—About—March—Halt—Dress.

Squadron! Left about Wheel.—March.—(Fig. 91.)

The standard faces about on his own centre, and the right half squadron wheels on him. The other half squadron wheels in like manner, but on a sliding pivot: for the rear-rank man on whom the wheel is made must stick close to the standard serjeant, who being in the rear-rank, of course shifts his ground in the wheel. Then the threes are wheeled up.

> The squadron will stand the depth of a rank further to the rear than before—the rank being between the dotted lines, as at R. The spaces between the lines B are the ground they have quitted. If the left half squadron, instead of wheeling on a sliding pivot, should wheel on the inner-flank man in his place, there would be two centres to the wheel; and of course the half squadron would not stand in the same line, but would stand (rear-ranks and front-ranks) on the spaces R and F *(Fig. 92.)* B B shewing the ground on which they before stood, and C C the two centres on which they have wheeled.
>
> Half squadrons or divisions may change front in the same manner. (Cav. Reg. ibid.)
>
> This is the best mode of changing the front of a squadron.

SECT. XCI.

The following methods of counter-marching the squadron are mentioned also in the Cavalry Regulations, Sect. 53:

The Squadron will counter-march by Files, from the Right (or Left) Flank.

Performed as by the divisions in Sect. 89.

> This takes too much room for general use.
>
> It may be done also by wheeling by twos or by threes to the flank, instead of filing.

SECT. XCII.

The Squadron will counter-march from the Right (or Left) Flank by Sub-divisions.

They break into a column of sub-divisions—the leading sub-division wheels about (by word from its own officer) and the others follow.

> This is open to the objections made above in Sect. 82. If done by divisions, it is freed from these objections, but requires more space.

SECT. XCIII.

The Squadron will counter-march on its Centre by Sub-divisions.

Left Half Squadron! By Threes—About—March.—Halt.

Half Squadrons! By Sub-divisions—Wheel inward.

The sub-division leaders conduct them forwards till the rear of each ~~column~~ has clear'd the standard: *Halt—Left wheel into line—March—Halt—Dress* (by the centre) and *Threes! Wheel up.* [*Fig. 94.*]

> It seems much easier to do this by divisions than by sub-divisions, on account of the shifting of the pivot-leaders.

SECT. XCIV.

The Squadron will change Front to the Rear, by the Wheels of Half-Squadrons.

Right Half Squadron! Forwards—(till advanced a little more than its own extent of front) *Halt.*

Half Squadrons! Wheel about inwards—March.

Right Half Squadron! Forwards—Halt—Dress.

PLATE XXII.

(The Column of Divisions marching right in Front.)

SECT. XCV.—Halt—Left Wing to the Front—March.

The leader of the rear division gives the word—*Threes! Right wheel—March*—then shifting to the right (now the front of the column of sixes) gives the word *Forwards*, just sufficiently to clear the flank of the column by a few paces, *Halt—Threes! Wheel up—March.—Halt—Eyes right—March*—and conducts them forward, remaining himself on the right (now the pivot) flank, and his coverer takes his place on the reverse flank.

As soon as he has passed the left centre-division, the leader of that division having previously wheeled by threes to the right, and shifted, leads his division down to cover the preceding division, wheels them up by threes, and follows. The remaining divisions in like manner, the pivots (now on the right) carefully covering, and conducted by their leaders. [*Fig.* 95.]

> The upper part of the figure is the column in its original position—the lower in its new position: the dotted lines shew the covering of the pivots, and the flank march of the divisions: the small letters signify, right, right centre – left centre, and left divisions.

> The pivots are now on a new alignement: if the old alignement is to be preserved, threes are wheeled to the left, and the divisions come out from the original pivot-flank (i. e. above, instead of below, in this figure.) Still the leaders must shift to the right-flank, and pivots cover.

> If it is required that the column remain on its own ground, the divisions, instead of waiting till passed, move forwards towards the rear. [Cav. Reg. Sect. 46.]

SECT. XCVI.

Fig. 96 describes a mode of counter-marching, by each division marching through the preceding divisions from rear to front. [Cav. Reg. Sect. 47.]

Left Division stand fast—Remaining Divisions! By Sub-divisions—Wheel about outwards—March. (By Squadron-officer.) Halt—Dress—(Given by Sub-division Leaders.)

March. (By Squadron-officer.)

The left division marches forwards, the remaining divisions also move forwards towards the rear, and as soon as the preceding division has passed, wheel about inwards and follow in open column: division-officers shifting to the right and coverers to the left. Eyes right, to the pivot-flank.

> By these means the column stands on its former ground. If that is not required, the sub-divisions instead of wheeling about, only passage outwards, and close in. [Cav. Reg. ibid.]

SECT. XCVII.

The Squadron will countermarch from both Flanks on its Centre. [Cav. Reg. Sect. 53.]

Threes! Wheel outward—March. (Squadron-officer.)

The flank-covering serjeants place their horses' heads towards the flanks to mark the ground—the right-flank marker by the front-rank, the left-flank marker by the rear-rank.

The flank-officers conduct the threes by left shoulders forward, about, close along by the rear, and front, as shewn in the dotted lines, till they come up to the markers. [*Fig.* 97.] Then " *Halt Threes! Wheel up.—Left Half Squadron! Forwards—Halt—Dress.*

> This may be done by twos, or by filing. [Cav. Reg. ibid.]

SECT. XCVIII.—Half Squadrons! To the Right Double.

If halted, the left half squadron reins back (dressing by the right) to an interval equal to its own front—passages in behind the right half squadron—is halted by its own flank officer, and dressed by the left flank, that being now the pivot. The right flank-officer shifts to the left flank.

Divisions! To the Right Double.

They rein back and passage in like manner by word from their own leaders—the division-officers shift to the pivots.

Pl.22.

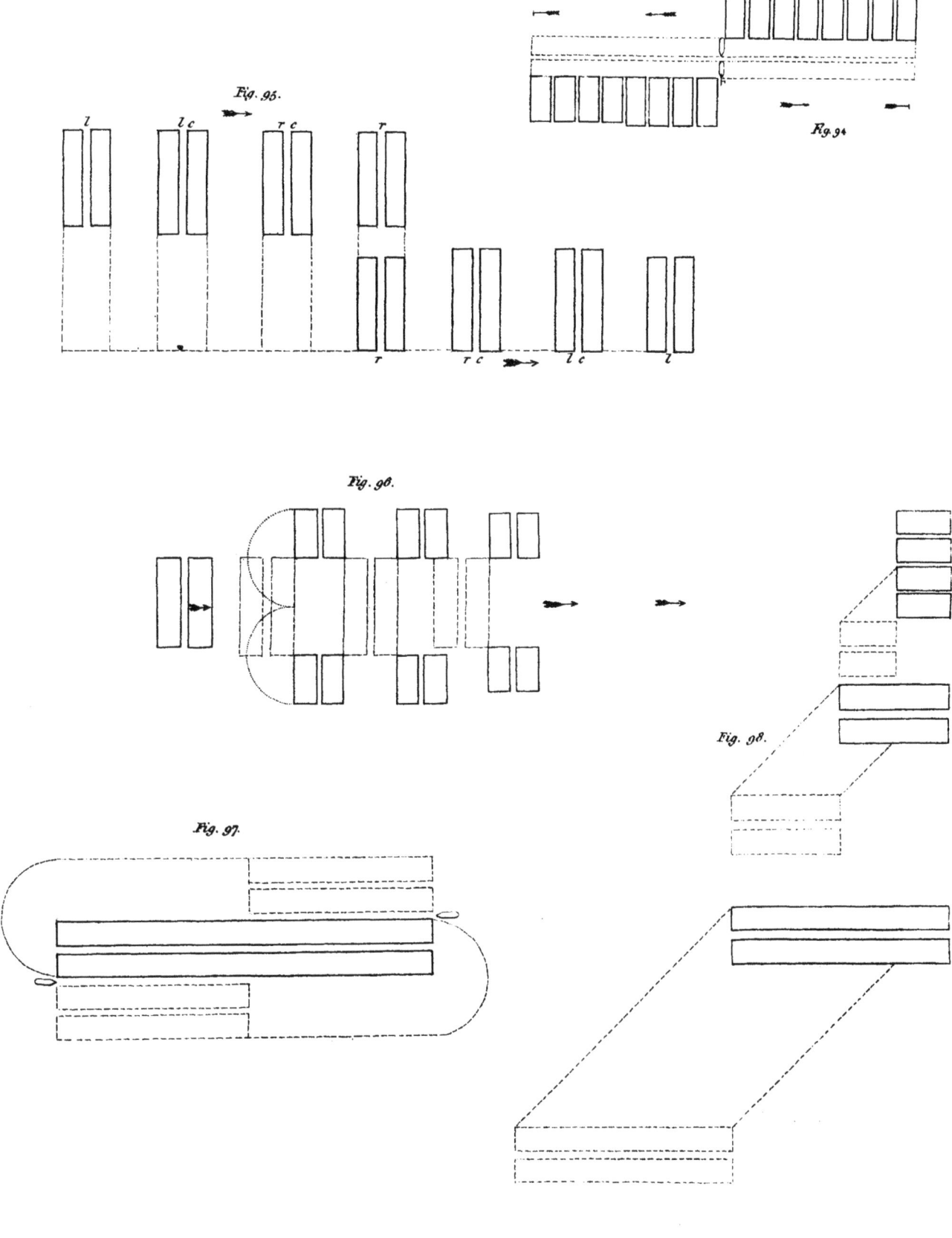

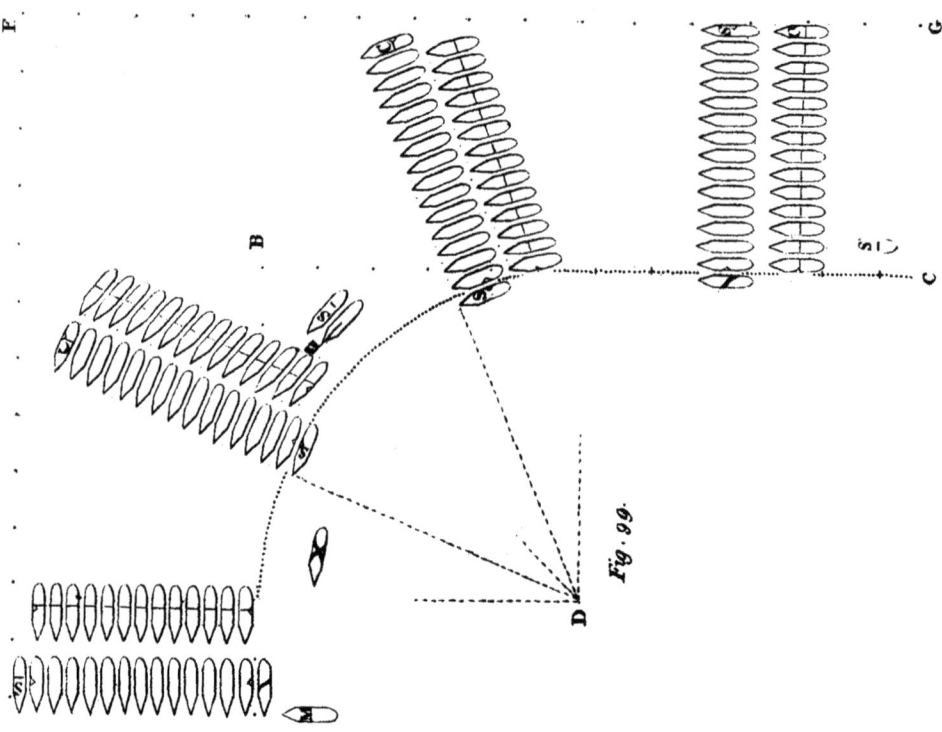

Pl. 23.

Fig. 99.

Fig. 100.

Sub-divisions! To the Right Double.

Performed in the same way.

If upon the march—the left half squadron, left division, or left sub-division, instead of reining back, halts (by word from its own officer): but the instant it has cleared the flank of the division on its right, inclines to the right till covering; and then receives (from the division officer) the word "*Forwards.*" The remaining divisions halt and incline, when they arrive on the same ground. [*Fig. 98.*]

The sub-division officers have time to shift, if done briskly.

This may be done, if so ordered, by all at the same instant, either from the halt, or upon the march.

> The column being in motion, it is impossible to represent it accurately in a drawing. But the inclined dotted lines shew the track made by the division while the preceding is moving from the ground now occupied by the doubling division. As the latter has more ground than the former to go over, (viz. both to flank and front) and must not lose its true interval, its march must be accelerated.

Form Divisions.

If on the march—LEFT INCLINE.

If halted—LEFT PASSAGE—MARCH—HALT—FORWARD—HALT—DRESS—*(By Sub-division Officer.)*

Form Half Squadrons.

The same—and words by division officers.

Form Squadrons.

The same—and word by left-flank officer.

The same must be done by doubling to the left, if the pivot is on the right; and forming will then be by passaging or inclining to the right.

> The doubling behind of half squadrons, divisions, &c. may be practised *by ranks*, i. e. the rear-rank first reining back to OPEN ORDER (an interval equal to the extent of their own front) then each left half-rank doubling behind the right half-rank. The word is—half ranks—divisions of ranks, or quarter ranks—sub-divisions, or eighths of ranks!—right double, &c. instead of—half squadrons, &c. (Cav. Reg. p. 286.) No shifting of officers.
>
> When at open order, they may be wheeled about outwards by half-ranks—halt—dress—and wheel about inwards – which tends to promote accuracy of wheeling: for if the pivots never quit their ground, the finding too much or too little room in wheeling up, shews the wheeling flanks exactly how much they have crouded in or loosened out.

PLATE XXIII.

Wheeling on sliding Pivots.

There are several points of distinction between wheeling on halted and on sliding pivots. In the former, the wheeling flank regulates the pace, and the other remains fixed; therefore during the wheel, eyes are directed to the wheeling flank; but at the instant of the halt, dressing is by the standing flank. In the latter, the pivot (whether it happens to be on the wheeling flank or not) regulates the pace and preserves the line of march; therefore the dressing must be during the whole time by the pivot flank, just as in the direct march of the column.

> The term "*pivot flank*" has been explained in page 27. If there is an apparent ambiguity here, when it is said that the *pivot* flank may or may not be the *wheeling* flank, and yet the evolution is called wheeling on a *sliding pivot*, it will be removed on recollecting, that by the "*pivot*-flank" is intended, *that on which they will wheel when wheeling into line*, not that flank on which a partial wheel may be made in column.

Another distinction is in the word of command. "*Right (or left) shoulders forward,*" is always to be given when the pivot continues the march. "*Right* shoulder forward" is equivalent to "*left* wheel," and *vice versâ*.

> Besides the directions given on this head in the Cavalry Regulations, the standing orders issued from the War-Office, January, 1799, notice that some regiments are not sufficiently attentive to the distinction between *shoulder forward* and *wheel*, and a strict conformity to the regulation in that particular is required.

SECT. XCIX.

Fig. 99—represents a column of divisions marching right in front (as in *Fig.* 87, *Plate* 21) and circling to the left by wheeling on sliding pivots. Markers are first sent forward to shew the new line of march.

> Three markers are necessary to direct the line of march of a column. Two of them being placed by the commanding officer in the intended line at the distance of about 150 yards from each other, the third rides briskly forward and at about 150 yards further, alignes himself upon them: i. e. he places himself so as to bring them into one point; the middle marker intercepting the outer ones from each other's sight. Their horses are placed parallel to each other and at right angles with the line. As soon as the head of the column approaches the first marker, (the first pivot leader preserving a line which passes close to the heads of the marker's horses) the first marker quits his ground, rides forward, and aligns himself in like manner upon the two others: and so each in succession prolonging the line, while the march of the column is to be direct.
>
> For entering upon new alignements, two additional markers are previously placed in the new line, and the ordinary markers (the first of which stands where the column is to enter) align themselves upom them.

The Column! Change direction. (given by the commanding officer.)

The leader of the first division at 20 or 30 yards from the point where the first marker stands, giving the word to his divifion

Right shoulders forward,

Leads them in the intended curve.

The leaders of the second and all the other divisions, keep their exact distance from their leading pivot, and follow exactly in his track, giving each the word "*Right fhoulders forward*" when on the ground where the first division wheeled: and each successively when arrived in the new line gives the word "*forwards*" and the column is in a right line again in the new direction.

> The small dotted curve shews the track of the pivots. The larger dots the old and new directions. C, B and G F the old— B, A and F E the new.
>
> If the ground should confine the flanks, it will be necessary to wheel on *halted* pivots at the point B; in which case the dressing must be instantaneous, or the wheeling division will not clear the ground in time for the succeeding division. Cav. Reg. page

If the change of direction is to the *right,* the leaders of divisions give the word

Left shoulders forward,

And circle themselves in a much larger curve to the right [*fig.* 100]. Eyes are still to the left. The pivots preserve their exact distances and tracks, and when arrived at the marker and in the new line, give the word "*forward*" each to his own division.

> In either of the above changes, the pivots are to preserve their exact pace: it follows, that when the pivot-flank is on the outer circle (as in *Fig.* 100) the reverse flank must slacken its pace: and when the pivot is on the inner circle, the reverse flank must accelerate its pace.
>
> The Cavalry Regulations speak of the leader circling *before* the line in the one case, leaving the point of intersection *within* his pivot hand, and in the other case of circling *behind* the line and leaving the point *without* the pivot hand. We must presume that by the *line* is meant the line in these figures, A, B, and by the point of intersection the angle A, B, C. But the lines E, F, and the angles E, F, G might with equal propriety be called so, and strictly speaking when an angle is cut off by any part of a circle, the *point of* intersection must *in all cafes,* be *without* the circle.
>
> In close column the flank on the outer circle must necessarily extend its interval, whether it be the pivot flank or the reverse flank.
>
> In these two figures the old and new lines form a right angle at the point of intersection—but any larger angle may be made when the change is less.

When the column marches left in front, the pivots being (as before is said) on the right, eyes are always to the right, both in left and right shoulders forward. These figures become inverted.

> We have before mentioned the necessity of filing as frequently from the left flank, as from the right. This observation will apply to all the manœuvres breaking into divisions, &c.
>
> It is easy after practising to the right, to understand *upon reflection* how the same movement is to be inverted and performed to the left: but it ought to become habitual and to be done *without* reflection, which can only be by practice.
>
> It also frequently happens that corps forming their squadron always on the same spot and to the same front, are apt to consider that as their proper front, and to be confused when it becomes changed; besides, by working in a parade ground somewhat confined in their flank marches, they are obliged to wheel at all the angles; and being usually formed at first with the rear near

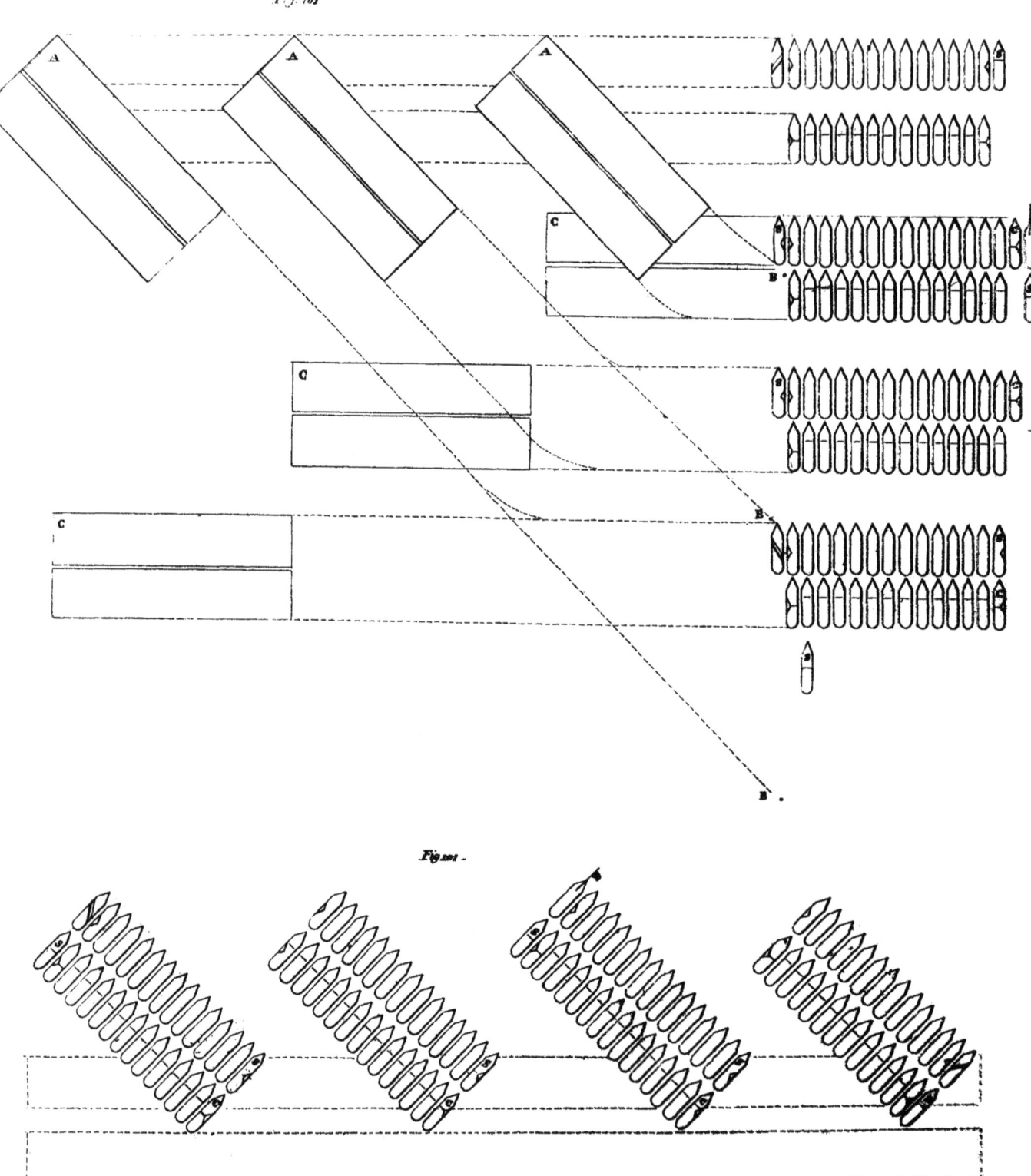

Fig. 102

Fig. 103

to the boundary of their ground, their pivot-flanks will be always within the circle, and their turns when the *right*-flank leads, will always be by *right* shoulders forward; and when the *left*-flank leads, by *left* shoulders forward. It will therefore be much better to form them occasionally on the same spot but with the front in the contrary direction, or sometimes to march them forwards in squadron to the opposite side of the ground, or countermarch or wheel the squadron *about*: in either of which cases on breaking into divisions and marching the column to a flank, the pivot-flank will be *without* the circle: of course, when the *right*-flank leads, the turns will be by *left* shoulders forward, and when the *left*-flank leads, by *right* shoulders forward.

PLATE XXIV.
ECHELLONS.

In breaking into echellons the divisions are separated at equal distances with parallel fronts, in the form of a step-ladder, as the word implies. The object of it is to disengage the flanks, so that the divisions may be able to march separately to either flank. The echellon is either direct or oblique. The former is formed, from line, by marching the divisions in different successive degrees to the front or rear; or from column, by marching them in the like manner to a flank. The latter is formed by wheeling the divisions on fixed pivots forwards or backwards less than the quarter circle.

The convenience and utility of the echellon position are very great. From the direct echellon the line is at once formed parallel to its former front, upon any named division, which stands fast, while the other divisions are marched to the front or rear till aligned upon it: or a column is formed in like manner by the *flank* march of the other divisions. From the oblique echellon the line is formed on any named division oblique to its former front: but the divisions must gain some ground to the flank, as their front and rear is partially intercepted by the flank of the preceding and following division. The close column is formed as from the former, and is oblique: an open column to the former flank is formed by wheeling up the divisions the residue of the whole quarter circle. The direct march also of the divisions when in oblique echellon answers the end of the inclined march of the line; and upon the halt they are in a situation to form oblique or parallel to their former line of front.

It is sufficient for the avowed intention of these pages to point out generally the powers of the echellon position, and the means of attaining it. For the particular methods of changing the front of the line, the reader is referred to the Cavalry Regulations.

SECT. C.

Fig. 101 represents the oblique echellon formed by a half wheel of the divisions to the right.

Squadron! by Divisions—to the Right, Half Wheel—March.

The wheel is marked by the right flank serjeant, as when breaking into column; but the pivot leaders do not shift, for the flank wheeled to is the directing flank; and if they are to form the line from this position, it must be by wheeling backwards on the same flank.

The echellon may be either of divisions or half squadrons: and any degree of wheel (as quarter, eighth, or sixteenth) may be made.

SECT. CI.

Fig. 102 describes the method of forming column in the rear of a flank division by the wheel backwards of the remaining divisions into oblique echellon.

In the Rear of the Right Division form open Column.

Right Division! Stand fast. Remaining Divisions! on your left half backwards.—Wheel.—March.

The parellelograms A A A are the divisions that have wheeled back. They are wheeled by threes to the right, and conducted by the division-officers till they arrive at the column-alignement B B B, then by right shoulders forward into their place in column, and threes wheeled up.

For a close column, a *quarter* wheel backwards is sufficient.

When one division stands fast, a wheel *forward* less than the whole quarter circle would not disengage the flanks. An eighth wheel backwards will just barely disengage the flanks of half squadrons; a quarter wheel, of divisions.

In wheeling backwards to the left, the front is presented to the right; and in order to avoid ambiguity arising from this circumstance, the word is *ON your left, backwards, wheel*: of course the wheel being made *on* the left, the left stands fast. Eyes are to the wheeling flank in the motion, and then immediately to the standing flank, as in wheeling forward.

In the elucidation of the Cavalry Regulations it is said that no markers are requisite in wheeling backwards.

When wheeled backwards upon any occasion, more than the half wheel, they must first go about by threes, then wheel forwards and threes wheel up. Caval. Reg. Sec. 24 and 25.

There is in the column (in this fig.) a space of a horse's length between the divisions; but when the rear ranks rein back to the close order interval upon dressing, it will be the true distance of close column, viz. half a horse's length between the divisions and between the ranks. Caval. Reg. page 141.

SECT. CII.

The same figure represents also a direct echellon of divisions formed by the deploying of the close column.

The parallelograms C C C describe it sufficiently without further explanation.

They may in like manner deploy and form squadron on any named division.

The Charge.

SECT. CIII. *Squadron! Centre—March.*

The squadron-officer marches directly forwards—the standard follows him exactly at the distance of one horse's length, the rest, front and rear, with eyes to the centre, advance in the direct line.

Trot (or bugle signal.)

It has been before mentioned, that the *close* of a bugle sound is the signal.

They strike at one and the same instant into a steady trot; carrying swords.

Gallop—(or bugle.)

They gallop steadily, square to the front—never pressing inwards though looking towards the centre—swords still carried.

Charge—(or bugle.)

They press forwards at somewhat more than three-quarters speed: body upright—swords at the position of *prepare,* and the attention at this instant at the utmost stretch, in order to preserve an even uniform front, and perfect direction.

Halt—(or bugle.)

The bodies of the riders at one instant thrown very much back, and the bridle hand raised to throw the horses well on their haunches. Swords sloped.

Halt—Dress.

Immediately after the first halt, the standard moves forwards a few paces, that all irregularities in the halt may be corrected without reining back, and all briskly dress up to him and halt.

They may retreat by "threes about"—by filing from both flanks to the rear; or in any way ordered.

Sometimes, during the charge, they are ordered to wheel-outward—or half-wheel outwards.

The half-squadrons opening outwards charge obliquely or directly along the supposed line of the enemy towards the flanks.

This is a rapid wheel on a sliding pivot. The wheeling flank is the pivot-flank; therefore eyes remain turned to it: and as the pace cannot be accelerated on the charge, the reverse flank must slacken pace and be careful not to crowd toward or press beyond the wheeling flank.

When this outward wheel is intended, the squadron should be informed of it before they advance; for during the impetuosity of the charge, an unexpected direction could not be followed by all instantaneously. They may wheel up into line, and close to the centre, or retreat by threes, and incline to the centre—or wheel to the right and left to the rear—or as may be ordered.

In advancing to the charge, the squadron-officer directs his sight towards the extremity of the ground intended for the charge, and marks several objects lying in the direct line; either strong and fixed objects beyond his intended point, or lesser objects which he cannot fail to find on the ground between his eye and that point; and thus is able to preserve the direct line that passes through such marked objects. To this and the pace his sole attention must be directed; for if he should look round to correct his squadron, he must swerve. The attention of the standard-officer, is to follow strictly his leader, and keep his interval. The eye of every individual is towards the centre, and his attention to the pace of his horse and perfect direction forwards, *yielding to pressure that comes from the centre—resisting pressure that comes from the flanks.* If he finds others before or behind him, by observing whether they are in line with the centre, he knows whether the fault is with them or himself, and continues or corrects his pace accordingly: making his corrections very gradually, or he will overdo it.

The charge is the most important of all the movements of cavalry. It is that for which all the evolutions are intended; for the main object of the whole of them is to produce with readiness an uniform front and in any given direction: but by constant attention to correct dressing in all the variety of positions and movements, of which a squadron is capable, the soldier learns to *dress* correctly in the charge: and although this matter, to such as have not considered the subject, may appear unimportant in itself, or essential only to parade, the fact is, that *in it the whole strength of cavalry consists*. The *momentum* producing the shock, is compounded of its weight and velocity: and its weight consists in its compactness. We may be excused for alluding to the fable of the bundle of sticks, which when together in a compact body, could not be broken, yet when separated yielded to a slight effort of strength.

It is next to impossible to describe all the variety of evolutions used in squadron; but it is hoped the general and fundamental principles have been sufficiently explained.

Where we have been too minute or even tedious, we must pray the reader's excuse: our aim has been perspicuity.

We feel confident that the able and experienced officers quoted in these pages, will not be offended at the few instances in which we may have presumed to criticise some of the less important parts of those works, for which the public is indebted to them: they wrote for persons already acquainted with the subject; and the first rudiments were not within their design.

The Cavalry Regulations contain instructions for officers in the higher parts of the duty required of them: this work is intended principally for the use of the privates, or to assist the officers in that part which may properly be termed *the drill*.

FINIS.

www.ingramcontent.com/pod-product-compliance
Ingram Content Group UK Ltd.
Pitfield, Milton Keynes, MK11 3LW, UK
UKHW050416240426
12048UKWH00021B/1545